J. D. Salinger and the Nazis

Staff Sergeant J. D. Salinger (L. Alsen artwork)

J. D. Salinger
and the Nazis

Eberhard Alsen

The University of Wisconsin Press

The University of Wisconsin Press
1930 Monroe Street, 3rd Floor
Madison, Wisconsin 53711-2059
uwpress.wisc.edu

3 Henrietta Street, Covent Garden
London WC2E 8LU, United Kingdom
eurospanbookstore.com

Printed in the United States of America

This book may be available in a digital edition.

Library of Congress Cataloging-in-Publication Data
Names: Alsen, Eberhard, author.
Title: J. D. Salinger and the Nazis / Eberhard Alsen.
Description: Madison, Wisconsin: The University of Wisconsin Press, [2018]
| Includes bibliographical references and index.
Identifiers: LCCN 2017044807 | ISBN 9780299315702 (cloth: alk. paper)
Subjects: LCSH: Salinger, J. D. (Jerome David), 1919–2010—Political and social
views. | Salinger, J. D. (Jerome David), 1919–2010—Criticism and
interpretation. | National socialism in literature.
Classification: LCC PS3537.A426 Z537 2018 | DDC 813/.54—dc23
LC record available at https://lccn.loc.gov/2017044807

Contents

Illustrations

Preface and Acknowledgments

J. D. Salinger came to prominence as a writer during the post–World War II renaissance of Jewish American literature. He stands out among other major writers of that movement—Saul Bellow, Philip Roth, and Bernard Malamud—because he deliberately avoided writing about Jewish themes. Above all, he avoided writing about the Holocaust even though he had seen what unspeakable atrocities the Nazis were capable of when he entered a recently abandoned concentration camp near the end of the war. In fact, there is only one reference to the Holocaust in all of his writings, including his wartime letters, and that reference is indirect.

Salinger's fiction shares with the work of Bellow, Roth, and Malamud such traits as a predilection for New York City locales; educated, middle-class characters; and the theme of people's alienation from the mainstream of American life. But it is hard to imagine that Bellow, Roth, or Malamud would have passed up the opportunity to write about the Holocaust if they had seen and smelled the still-smoldering corpses of scores of Jewish prisoners whose quarters the SS had set on fire.

There are complicated reasons for Salinger's unwillingness to confront the Holocaust. Among them are his upbringing, his adversarial attitude toward the US Army, and his nervous breakdown shortly after the end of the war. These factors made him change his attitude toward the Nazis from an early unconcern, to a gung-ho "Kill the Nazis" attitude, and from there to a final nonjudgmental stance.

This book developed out of research I did for Shane Salerno's 2013 film *Salinger* and for the massive oral biography that accompanied it. I am very grateful to

Mr. Salerno for funding research trips to archives in the United States and Germany. I am especially grateful that Mr. Salerno gave me permission to use this research in my book. Necessarily some of the material in my book overlaps with that in the chapters of Mr. Salerno's biography, where it deals with Salinger's concentration camp experience and his German wife. But the most important ideas I present—especially the reasons Salinger came to feel non-judgmental toward the Nazis and hostile toward the US Army—do not appear in Mr. Salerno's book and movie.

Concerning my research in Europe, I want to express my gratitude to three archivists and two journalists who provided me with valuable information. The archivists are Jürgen Zottman of the Nuremberg city archive; Reiner Kammerl, who heads the town of Weißenburg archive; and Lukas Morscher of the Stadtarchiv Innsbruck in Austria. I am also grateful to the freelance journalist Bernd Noack, who published new information about Salinger's time in Germany in the *Frankfurter Allgemeine Zeitung,* and especially to Jan Stephan of the newspaper *Weißenburger Tagblatt,* who allowed me to use information from an as-yet-unpublished interview with two relatives of Salinger's German wife.

Additional thanks go to Norbert Hofmann of the University of Tübingen; to Sarah Elbert, formerly at Cornell University; and to Raphael Kadushin of the University of Wisconsin Press. They read an earlier version of the book and offered excellent advice.

J. D. Salinger and the Nazis

Introduction

J. D. Salinger's attitude toward the Nazis is a topic that has not yet been explored. This is surprising because during World War II Salinger's job as an agent of the Counter Intelligence Corps (CIC) was to arrest Nazi spies and collaborators, and after the war he continued to work for the CIC as a private investigator, tracking down Nazis who had gone into hiding.

I became interested in Salinger's attitude toward the Nazis when I ran across two pieces of biographical information in *Dream Catcher*, a memoir by his daughter, Margaret. One was the fact that near the end of the war Salinger entered a recently abandoned concentration camp and saw the dead bodies of hundreds of Jewish prisoners. The other was that the woman Salinger married right after the war was German and not French as had been widely believed. Moreover, Margaret claimed that this woman had been a minor official of the Nazi Party. So my first reason for doing the research for this book was to find an explanation for Salinger marrying a German woman even though he was a Holocaust witness.

A second reason for writing this book was to find out why Salinger, who grew up in a Jewish family, did not mention the Holocaust in any of his stories and why he deals with Jewish themes in only two of his thirty-five published stories.

A third reason was that I wanted to correct a widely accepted piece of misinformation about Salinger's military service. He was an agent of the Counter Intelligence Corps and not a combat soldier. Contrary to what the most recent biographies claim, the daily reports of Salinger's commanding officer show that his CIC detachment never participated in combat.

Finally, I had a personal reason for studying Salinger's attitude toward the Nazis. My father was a Nazi, and I myself was subjected to Nazi indoctrination when I was a child.

My father, Karl Alsen, was a member of the paramilitary Sturmabteilung (SA) from 1933 to 1935, a member of the Nazi Party from 1937 to 1938, and an officer in the German army, the Wehrmacht, from 1938 to 1945. He spent most of the war years with the German occupation forces in Bordeaux, France. A desk soldier in the Quartermaster Corps, he enjoyed his time in Bordeaux and got along well with the French because he loved French culture and spoke fluent French.

While doing the research for this book, I learned that it was Salinger's Twelfth Infantry Regiment that took my father prisoner at the end of the war. My father told me that during the last days of the war he had been put in command of a number of dispersed units near Bad Tölz in southern Bavaria. A bureaucrat, he had never commanded troops, but there were very few officers left at the end of the war. On May 4, 1945, when he tried to surrender the troops assigned to him, an American patrol machine-gunned his jeep, killing his driver and taking my father prisoner.

From the combat history of the Twelfth Infantry Regiment, I learned that on May 4 and 5, 1945, the regiment was rounding up Wehrmacht soldiers by the hundreds in the Bad Tölz area. On May 5, the day following my father's capture, "twelve German trucks loaded with enemy soldiers drove into the [Twelfth Regiment's] column to surrender."[1] These must have been the ragtag troops under my father's command.

Amazed by the coincidence, I sent Salinger my father's picture and his Wehrmacht ID papers (*Soldbuch*), and I asked him if he, Salinger, was part of the CIC team that interrogated my father. Salinger responded: "Can only tell you that it is most improbable that I might have known or known of your father. His surely valued photograph and Army record-book are enclosed in this envelope."[2]

I found Salinger's response puzzling at first. But then I learned from CIC manuals that enemy soldiers of officer rank could be interrogated only by American officers. This means that Salinger could not have questioned my father because Salinger was not an officer but a staff sergeant, and my father was a lieutenant colonel.

And here is the story of my own indoctrination with Nazi ideas. My father had nothing to do with it because for most of the war he was stationed in France. When I was five years old, our house in Nuremberg was bombed out, and my mother and I were evacuated to the Sudetenland, the German-speaking part of what was then Czechoslovakia. There I began to attend a kindergarten in the

Lieutenant Colonel Karl Alsen (Alsen family photo)

small town of Tachau (now Tachow in the Czech Republic). In that kindergarten I had to say a Nazi prayer every morning. It was an old Catholic prayer with the name of Jesus Christ replaced by the name of Adolf Hitler:

> Händchen falten
> Köpfchen senken
> Und an Jesus Christus denken.
>
> [Fold your little hands
> Bow your little head
> And think of Adolf Hitler.]

My mother was upset when she found out about the prayer. As she told me later, there was nothing she could have done about it without attracting the attention of the Gestapo (the secret state police). But she was even more horrified when she found out that the kindergarten teachers had told me to greet all adults I met in the street by raising my right arm in the Nazi salute and shouting "Heil Hitler." To this my mother responded by saying that while I was in the kindergarten, I had to do what the teachers told me, but on my way home I had to do what *she* told me. And she told me not to do the Hitler salute. That was in the fall of 1944.

Fifteen years later, I did my required military service in the postwar German Army, the Bundeswehr, which was still using weapons from World War II. For instance, we were trained on the MG 34 and the MG 42, the two standard machine guns of the Wehrmacht. And some of us got to fire blanks with the 81 mm mortar that plays an important role in Salinger's story "The Stranger."

But not all our weapons came from the Wehrmacht; some came from the US Army. For instance, the handgun we were issued was the same .45 caliber M1911 A1 that Salinger carried, the gun he was thinking of using to a fire a bullet through his left hand when he had his nervous breakdown.

As I studied Salinger's attitude toward the Nazis, I was astonished to find how rarely the word Nazi appears in his stories and wartime letters, even though his job as a CIC agent confronted him every day with Nazi spies and collaborators and later with members of the SS and the Nazi Party. In fact, he uses the word in only three of his works of fiction and in only one of his letters from abroad.

The word *Nazi* has two different meanings. In "For Esmé—With Love and Squalor" it refers to a member of the Nazi Party, such as the one arrested by the central character, Sergeant X. And in a 1945 letter from Germany, Salinger

Basic training with the MG 34 machine gun (Alsen family photo)

mentions that he has signed a postwar contract with the CIC to "hunt Nazis" who have gone into hiding. In both of these cases the word *Nazi* refers to a member of the Party, the Nationalsozialistische Deutsche Arbeiterpartei. But in "Last Day of the Last Furlough" and in *The Catcher in the Rye*, Salinger calls all German soldiers Nazis. This use of the term was common among American, British, and Canadian troops in World War II.

Strictly speaking, though, German soldiers were not Nazis because members of the Wehrmacht were not allowed to be in the Nazi Party. Still, it made sense to call them Nazis because even after the war was over many continued to identify with the Nazi regime. This has been shown by Felix Römer, who examined clandestine CIC recordings of conversations among some ten thousand German prisoners of war at Fort Hunt, Virginia. These recording indicate that while some Wehrmacht soldiers rejected the Nazi ideology, "the majority stood behind Hitler even far into the last year of the war" because "to fight for the Nazi system had become part of their flesh and blood."[3]

In this book, I discuss sixteen Salinger stories, *The Catcher in the Rye*, and thirteen unpublished wartime letters. The stories and the novel all contain characters who were soldiers in the US Army during World War II, and they all reveal — directly or indirectly — Salinger's attitude toward the Nazis.

As I read through Salinger's wartime stories, it struck me how different they are from Hemingway's war stories and novels (*In Our Time*, 1925; *A Farewell to Arms*, 1929; *For Whom the Bell Tolls*, 1940) and from the World War II novels of the German Nobel laureate Heinrich Böll (*The Train Was on Time*, 1949; *And Where Were You, Adam*, 1951). Unlike Hemingway and Böll, Salinger never shows his characters actually firing their weapons, even though some of them come under fire from the enemy. This peculiarity of Salinger's wartime stories is obviously due to the fact that he was not a combat soldier.

Finally, I want to offer an explanation of the material I analyzed and of the way I structured this book. I focus primarily on Salinger's early fiction, published and unpublished; on unpublished letters; and on oral statements Salinger made that relate to his attitude toward the Nazis. I also quote from the daily reports of Salinger's CIC detachment, from other military records, and from several military histories.

I organized the book chronologically in terms of the events in Salinger's life as reflected in the stories, and I begin each chapter by establishing the historical and biographical context of the stories. Two special cases are "A Girl I Knew" and "For Esmé—With Love and Squalor." Both have a first part that takes place before D-Day and a second part that takes place after the war. I discuss the biographical content of these stories first in the context of Salinger's experiences before the D-Day invasion and again later in the context of Salinger's experiences during and after the war.

1

A Secular Jewish Upbringing

Jerome David Salinger sprang from Jewish and Catholic stock. His father's ancestors came from Poland and his mother's from Germany. His father, Solomon Salinger, was born in Cleveland, Ohio, and his mother, Marie Jillich, a Catholic, was born in Athens, Iowa. In 1910 the two were married in Chicago, where Solomon was the manager of a movie theater. To appease Solomon's Jewish family, Marie changed her name to Miriam and pretended to have converted to Judaism.

After the movie theater went out of business, Solomon found a job with the J. S. Hoffman Company of Chicago, famous for importing cheeses and hams from Europe. Solomon's willingness to work for that company signals that he was not an observant Jew. Had he been, he would not have wanted to have anything to do with hams, one of the most nonkosher foods. Solomon made himself so useful to HofCo that they put him in charge of the New York City branch of the company less than two years after he started working for them. So in 1912, shortly after their first child, Doris, was born, the Salingers moved to Manhattan.

Because of his talent in business, Solomon eventually wound up vice president of HofCo. His financial success is illustrated by the fact that the Salinger family moved their Manhattan home four times, each time to a more upscale neighborhood. They finally wound up at 1133 Park Avenue, where their second child, Jerome David (nicknamed "Sonny"), spent most of his youth. This was an imposing fourteen-story building whose apartments all had servants' quarters. Like the other tenants—all of them probably white, Anglo-Saxon Protestants—the Salingers employed a live-in maid.

Solomon and Miriam apparently tried to fit in with their wealthy WASP neighbors. This may be why, shortly after the family's move to Park Avenue,

1133 Park Avenue, where Salinger grew up (L. Alsen photo)

Solomon told his son and daughter that they were not really Jewish. Salinger's daughter, Margaret, heard the story from her Aunt Doris: "When Doris was nearly twenty, shortly after Sonny's bar mitzvah, their parents told them that they weren't *really* Jewish. Their mother, Miriam, was actually named Marie, and she had been 'passing' as a Jew since her marriage to Sol."[1] Solomon had decided to go by the name of Sol, apparently because he did not want to be immediately recognized as Jewish. Similarly, his son did not want to draw attention to his Jewishness with his given name Jerome and published all of his fiction under the name J. D. Salinger. Sonny's bar mitzvah was probably only to please Sol's Jewish family.

In short, Sol and Miriam Salinger were not religious Jews. As Margaret explains: "I knew that my father did not attend Jewish religious services as a child and that his family, in fact, celebrated Christmas, so I assumed, even after I had learned that he had grown up thinking he was Jewish, that their sense of belonging to the Jewish community was limited. In fact, I found out that the Salinger family's lack of religious attendance was not unusual. In 1929, approximately 80 percent of Jewish youth in New York City were found to have had no religious training at all."[2]

The Salingers were trying to assimilate into upper-class Gentile society. For instance, after Sonny had struggled through a number of Manhattan public schools, his parents decided to send him to a private school for his secondary schooling. They chose the McBurney School, which was associated with the Young Men's Christian Association. And when Sonny flunked out of McBurney's, they picked a WASP military prep school, the Valley Forge Military Academy in Pennsylvania.

Biographer Ian Hamilton examined the Valley Forge application that Sol Salinger filled out, and he reports that there are "irritated horizontal scratchings of the pen when asked about his son's religion—the answer appears to have been none."[3] Even though Sol Salinger signed the application form, he decided not to accompany his wife and his son to the application interview. Hamilton notes, "Sol himself chose not to make the trip. And when, shortly afterward, Valley Forge sent a lieutenant to New York to conclude the deal (Valley Forge, like most other schools in 1934, was desperately short of funds), it was Mrs. Salinger with whom he dealt, not Sol."[4] After all, with her fair complexion and auburn hair Miriam definitely did not look Jewish. So by having Miriam do the negotiations with Valley Forge, Sol was trying to help his son pass. Margaret Salinger writes that Sol coming to Valley Forge with Sonny would have been the equivalent of the boy showing up there wearing "a great big sign on his backside that said, 'Kick me, I'm Jewish.'"[5]

It is possible that Sol's unwillingness to own up to his Jewishness was a reaction to the anti-Semitism that was rampant in the 1920s and 1930s, but it also seems that he and his family were embarrassed to be Jewish. Margaret Salinger reports that "the whole subject of Jewishness is something my father is very touchy about indeed."[6]

One example that shows how touchy J. D. Salinger was about his Jewishness has to do with his financial support of a small group of Hasidic Jews for whom he felt "real affection." But that affection evaporated when they sent him a letter that profoundly offended him. Here is how Margaret reports her father's response: "He said he even sent them a little money from time to time, because they were quite poor. In the letter he was holding, the rebbe had asked him what was his mother's maiden name. 'I'll cut them off,' he said, slashing the air with his hand. 'I'll never speak to them again.'"[7] The rebbe probably did not mean any harm, but Salinger apparently felt that the rebbe was questioning his Jewishness and wanted to know if he was a real Jew or only half a Jew.

This was one instance when J. D. Salinger was unable to turn the embarrassing subject of his Jewishness into a joke, which was what he usually did. For example, he was mortified by his grandfather Simon Salinger, who had "a loud, embarrassing Yiddish accent." But he made his grandfather's accent into a joke when he told the story of riding on a bus with him. As Margaret tells it, "My father, then a young boy, nearly died of embarrassment as his grandfather called out each street number on the Madison Avenue bus they were riding. 'Forty-feef Street, Forty-seex Street,' my father would call out in a loud voice with a heavy Yiddish accent as he told the story."[8]

It's one thing to share your embarrassment with your family, but it's quite another thing to be embarrassed in front of outsiders. And if you are embarrassed about your Jewishness, one way to avoid embarrassment is to avoid talking or writing about things Jewish.

Of the thirty-five stories Salinger published, only two have Jewish themes. I will discuss "Down at the Dinghy" here because it relates to Salinger's upbringing, and I will discuss "A Girl I Knew" in a later chapter because it relates to Salinger's postwar experiences.

"Down at the Dinghy" was first published in the *New Yorker* in April 1949 and later reprinted in *Nine Stories* (1953). The central character is Beatrice "Boo Boo" Tannenbaum, one of the seven children of the Glass family. The Glasses are a part-Jewish family like the Salingers, with the father, Les Glass, being Jewish and the mother, Bessie Glass, being Irish Catholic. But the Glasses are even less Jewish than the Salingers because none of the four boys was barmitzvahed. Instead one son converted to Catholicism and became a Carthusian monk, and the rest of the children were tutored in Vedanta Hinduism by their oldest brother, Seymour. None of this information appears in "Down at the Dinghy," but it resonates through the story for those who have read the other six segments of the composite novel about the Glass family.[9]

That the theme of "Down at the Dinghy" is anti-Semitism becomes apparent only on the last page. Here is what happens: Boo Boo's four-year-old son, Lionel, has run away from home again, but only as far as the small sailboat that is tied up at the family's dock. When Boo Boo goes to bring Lionel home and asks him why he ran away, he tells her that he overheard a conversation between the family's maid, Sandra, and Mrs. Snell, a woman who does their laundry:

"Sandra—told Mrs. Smell [*sic*]—that Daddy's a big—sloppy—kike." So Boo Boo asks Lionel: "Do you know what a kike is, baby?" And Lionel answers: "It's one of those things that go up in the *air*—With *string* you hold." Boo Boo doesn't pursue the matter. Instead she tells Lionel that they will go into town, buy some pickles and bread, and eat them in the car. Then they'll pick up his daddy from the train and "make him take us for a ride in the boat. You'll have to help him carry the sails down. O.K.?" The story ends with these sentences: "They didn't walk back to the house, they raced. Lionel won."[10]

Aside from its theme of anti-Semitism, the story is all about avoidance. The concept comes across in three different ways, most obviously in Boo Boo's avoidance of giving her too young son an explanation of the anti-Semitic epithet *kike*, and also in Lionel's running away from something that he senses is nasty. The image on Lionel's sweatshirt refers to avoidance as well. It is a picture of "Jerome the Ostrich playing the violin." Rather than sticking his head in the sand to avoid something unpleasant as ostriches supposedly do (a cliché that misrepresents the habits of ostriches), Jerome the ostrich plays the violin. His playing the violin hints at another cliché, namely that of Nero fiddling while Rome burned (also not based in fact). And the name *Jerome* suggests that the ostrich is J. D. Salinger. Thus the image of violin-playing Jerome the ostrich can be read as Salinger's sly acknowledgement of his habit of avoiding themes that are troubling (for instance, the Holocaust) and instead fiddling with less important topics.[11]

2

Salinger in Austria
before the Nazi Takeover

In 1937 and 1938, young Jerry Salinger spent ten months in Austria and Poland, mostly in Vienna. In his book *J. D. Salinger: A Life*, Kenneth Slawenski asserts that during his time in Vienna, Salinger witnessed Nazis forcing Jews "to scrub the gutters" of Vienna streets.[1] But these acts of barbarism occurred after Salinger had already left Austria. In the story "A Girl I Knew" (1948) an alter ego of Salinger's also spent some time in Austria before the Nazi takeover, and like Salinger, he did not find out what the Nazis were doing to the Jews in Vienna until after he got home to the United States.

The facts of the matter are these: When eighteen-year-old Jerry Salinger flunked out of New York University in the spring of 1937, his father, Sol Salinger, decided to apprentice him to the ham importing business. To that end, he sent him to Europe so he could improve his German to the point where he would be able to write German advertisements for his father's company. Because of the well-known anti-Semitism of the Nazis who were running the German government, Sol sent his son not to Germany but to Austria.

But in March 1938, Sol made Jerry return to the United States because of the imminent takeover of Austria by the German army. Jerry left Le Havre on board the French steamer *Île de France* on March 9, 1938, and he arrived back in New York on March 16. While Salinger was on his way home, on March 12, 1938, Hitler's troops marched into Vienna and made Austria part of Nazi Germany.

It is a little known fact that Austria had already been a fascist country before the German Nazis took over. Since May 1934, Austria had been ruled by one political party, the Fatherland Front. All other parties, including the Austrian

The Nazis roll into Vienna (German Bundesarchiv)

Nazi Party, were barred from participation in the government. But the agenda of the Fatherland Front did not include sanctions against Jews or other minorities in multiethnic Austria.

In July 1934, the Austrian Nazi Party made an unsuccessful attempt to replace the Fatherland Front. During this abortive coup, they assassinated Austrian chancellor Engelbert Dollfuss. The Austrian authorities jailed scores of Nazis and outlawed the Nazi Party. But in July 1936, the government of Dollfuss's successor, Chancellor Kurt Schuschnigg, caved in to pressure from Nazi Germany and issued an amnesty for most of those who had been involved in the failed coup d'état of 1934. As a result, the Austrian Nazi Party was able to regroup, and its leaders immediately fell in line with the anti-Semitic propaganda of the German Nazi Party. Then in early 1938, Hitler threatened to invade Austria unless Schuschnigg handed power over to the Austrian Nazis. Schuschnigg resigned on March 11, 1938. The next day, the Wehrmacht invaded Austria.[2]

Because the Schuschnigg government had kept the Austrian Nazis in check, the Jewish population had been safe until the country was swallowed up by Germany. Before he resigned, Schuschnigg had ordered a national referendum on whether Austria was to become part of Germany. Of course, Hitler canceled that referendum after the Wehrmacht took control of the country. Nevertheless, supporters of Schuschnigg's Fatherland Front painted the emblem

Nazis force Jews to scrub Fatherland Front slogans off sidewalks (Yad Vashem Museum, Jerusalem)

of their party and anti-Nazi slogans on the sidewalks of Vienna's downtown shopping streets. The Nazis reacted by randomly rounding up Jews and making them scrub those images and slogans off the sidewalks. The *New York Times* ran two articles on that story. On the day Salinger arrived back in the United States, a *New York Times* headline read, "Jews Humiliated by Vienna Crowds. Families Compelled to Scrub Streets." And a week later a *New York Times* headline stated, "Jews Scrub Streets of Vienna Inner City. Forced to Remove Crosses of Fatherland Front."[3]

Salinger apparently did not learn what Nazism was all about during his time in Austria and Poland because he did not refer to the Nazis in any of his published comments about his stay in Europe. It was not until 1944 that he referred to Hitler and the Nazis in one of his stories. That story is "Last Day of the Last Furlough." And it was not until 1948, ten years after his return from Austria, that Salinger worked his experiences in Vienna into "A Girl I Knew."

The first published reference to Salinger's stay in Europe occurred three years after his return to the United States in a note titled "Backstage at *Esquire*." The occasion was the publication of "The Heart of a Broken Story" in *Esquire* magazine. According to that note, "He visited pre-Anschluss Vienna when he was eighteen, winning high honors in beer hoisting. In Poland, he worked in a ham factory and slaughter house."[4]

In a "Contributors" note for *Story* magazine in 1942, Salinger offered this account of his stay in Vienna and Poland: "Spent a year in Europe when I was eighteen and nineteen, most of the time in Vienna. . . . I was supposed to apprentice myself to the Polish ham business. . . . They finally dragged me off to Bydgoszcz for a couple of months, where I slaughtered pigs, wagoned through the snow with the big slaughter-master, who was determined to entertain me by firing his shotgun at sparrows, light bulbs, fellow employees."[5]

Salinger's next reference to his prewar experiences in Europe is a one-sentence statement in a 1945 letter to Ernest Hemingway. At the time Salinger was stationed with the US Army of Occupation in Germany, and he told Hemingway that he hoped the army would send him to Vienna, where he wanted "to put a pair of ice skates on the feet of a Viennese girl again."[6]

The last reference to Salinger's stay in Austria and Poland appeared in a 1951 biographical note that he authorized his friend William Maxwell to publish in the *Book of the Month Club News*. The piece was part of an advertisement for *The Catcher in the Rye*:

> In the middle of his college period, his father sent him to Europe for a year to learn German and to write ads for a firm that exported Polish hams. It was a happy year. He lived in Vienna with an Austrian family, and learned some German and a good deal about people, if not about the ham exporting business. Eventually he got to Poland and for a brief while he went with a man at four o'clock in the morning and bought and sold pigs.[7]

The only reference to the Nazis in the published statements about Salinger's time in Austria occurs in the 1941 contributors note for *Esquire*. The editor who wrote the note used the term *Anschluss*, the Nazis' euphemism for their annexation of Austria. But Salinger himself never referred to what the Nazis were doing to the Jews in Austria until after the war, when he wrote "A Girl I Knew."

"A Girl I Knew" has more autobiographical content than any other Salinger story because the narrator—who identifies himself only by his first name, John—has a lot in common with Salinger. In the prewar part of the story John is a thin boy of six foot two, just like young Salinger was. His father sends him to Vienna to apprentice him to his business and to learn German. He has aspirations as a writer and writes juvenile plays—exactly what Salinger did at the time. But the crucial part of the story concerns John's relationship with a pretty Jewish girl named Leah whose family lives in the same apartment building, a level below

John's host family. This also seems to be based on fact because Salinger had a crush on a Viennese girl. And in the postwar part of the story we learn that, like Salinger, John had been a Counter Intelligence Corps agent.

The story of Leah begins when she agrees to give John lessons in German conversation. He immediately falls in love with her, but he soon discovers that she is engaged to a young man from Poland. When John's time in Vienna is up, he is distressed that he cannot say goodbye to Leah because she happens to be in Warsaw with her future in-laws. All John can do is send Leah a hilarious goodbye letter in fractured German.

There is an intriguing difference between the time frames of Salinger's and John's stays in Vienna. Salinger was in Vienna from May 1937 to March 1938, but he decided to date John's time in Vienna a year earlier and to make it shorter: John arrives in Vienna in July 1936 and leaves five months later, in December of that year.

After pondering this change in dates for a while, I have come to the conclusion that it has to do with the Nazi takeover of Austria on March 12, 1938. I believe that Salinger made the events in part one of "A Girl I Knew" take place a year earlier than his own stay in Europe because he wanted to avoid having to mention the Nazis in the early part of the story. John, the narrator of "A Girl I Knew," does not learn about the Nazi takeover of Austria until he has gone back to college over a year after his return from Vienna.

Although John does not mention the Nazis where he recounts his experiences in Vienna, he makes up for it in the part of the story that occurs after he is back home. He starts off that part with a Holden Caulfield–style fantasy of killing Nazis.

> About the same hour Hitler's troops were marching into Vienna, I was on reconnaissance for Geology 1-b, searching perfunctorily, in New Jersey, for a limestone deposit. But during the weeks and months that followed the German take-over of Vienna, I often thought of Leah. Sometimes just thinking of her wasn't enough. When, for example, I had examined the most recent newspaper photographs of Viennese Jewesses on their hands and knees scrubbing sidewalks, I quickly stepped across my dormitory room, opened a desk drawer, slipped an automatic into my pocket, then dropped noiselessly from my window to the street, where a long-range monoplane, equipped with a silent engine, awaited my gallant, foolhardy, hawk-like whim.[8]

John's concern about Leah is kept alive when he receives a package and a letter from her. The package contains two gramophone records that she and John used to listen to in Vienna and that he had accidentally left behind. In the letter, Leah tells him that she is now married and living in Vienna. Since Leah forgot to put a return address on the package, John cannot get in touch with her and find out how she and her family are doing under Nazi rule.

Like John, Salinger went back to college after his return from Austria. The story doesn't tell us how successful John was in college, but Salinger lasted only one semester. During this time, the fall of 1938, Salinger was less concerned about the Nazi takeover of Austria than was John in "A Girl I Knew." Unlike John, Salinger did not spend the weeks and months that followed the German takeover worrying about the Jewish girl he had a crush on in Vienna.

The college Salinger attended was Ursinus College in Pennsylvania, not far from Valley Forge Military Academy, where he had received his secondary schooling. At Ursinus he practiced his writing by doing a column titled The Skipped Diploma for the college paper, the *Ursinus Weekly*. Recurring headings were "Movie Dept.," "Theater Dept.," "Book Dept.," and "Campus Dept." In the column Salinger discussed recent movies, plays, and books, and indulged in campus gossip and criticism of academic life. Nowhere in those pieces did he mention Hitler or the Nazis' treatment of the Jews in Austria.

But one of Salinger's classmates did refer to Hitler in the *Ursinus Weekly*. On October 10, 1938, the author of a column called "Gaff" quoted a "senior practice teacher" as saying, "Hitler won't fight but my class will."[9] This is probably a reference to news of the so-called Munich Peace Agreement. On September 30, 1938, British prime minister Neville Chamberlain had reported that in his negotiations with Hitler, he had secured "peace for our time" by agreeing to let the Nazis annex the German-speaking part of Czechoslovakia and by making Hitler sign a treaty promising not to attack the rest of the country.

The closest the nineteen-year-old Salinger came to showing any interest in international politics is in a piece in the *Ursinus Weekly* about an antiwar speech that President Franklin Delano Roosevelt had given two years earlier. The most famous section of that speech begins with the words "I have seen war" and ends with the words "I hate war." In his column The Skipped Diploma, Salinger offers a mini-play poking fun at Roosevelt and having him plagiarize Civil War general William Tecumseh Sherman's famous phrase "War is hell." Here is that four-line mini-play:

> FRANKLIN: I hate war. Eleanor hates war. James, Franklin, Elliott, and
>   John hate war. Sissie and Buzzie hate war. War is hell! . . . . How does
>   that sound, Eleanor?
> ELEANOR: Mm-hmmm. . . .[10]

There are two possible reasons Salinger was less interested than some of his classmates in what the Nazis were up to in Europe. One reason might be that he had developed an intense ambition to become a literary artist. Another student at Ursinus, Frances Thierolf, remembers that Salinger told her he hoped that one day he would write the "Great American Novel." Frances also told biographer Ian Hamilton that Salinger came across as a "handsome, suave, and sophisticated New Yorker" and that "most girls were mad about him at once."[11] This comment hints at a second possible reason Salinger paid no attention to the Nazis while he was at Ursinus College: his fascination with girls.

Salinger's preoccupation with girls is illustrated in his first published story, "The Young Folks." The story takes place at a student party, and the central character is the unattractive Edna Phillips. She lures the fingernail-biting Bill Jameson out onto the dark balcony and tries to make him feel romantic about her. But Bill disentangles himself with the excuse that he has to write a paper for a Monday class. When the hostess of the party asks Edna how she and Bill got along, Edna claims that Bill tried to get fresh with her: "I'm still in one piece. Only keep that guy away from me, willya?"[12] The story captures the atmosphere of 1940s college parties, and it suggests that during his time at Ursinus College, Salinger was more interested in exploring the psyche of the female of the species than in following accounts of the Nazis terrorizing Jews in Austria.

Salinger left Ursinus College after the Fall 1938 semester and returned to New York to take a short story writing course at Columbia University. That course was taught by Whit Burnett, the founder and editor of the literary magazine *Story*. Burnett wound up becoming Salinger's mentor.

Burnett and his first wife, Mary Foley, had founded *Story* magazine back in 1931 in Vienna. After the Nazis rose to power in Germany in 1933, the Burnetts transplanted themselves and their magazine to New York City. *Story* flourished because Burnett had an uncanny ability to recognize up-and-coming talent. Among the writers Burnett featured in his magazine were Richard Wright, Tennessee Williams, John Cheever, and Joseph Heller.

Salinger took Burnett's short story course two semesters in a row (spring and fall of 1939), and in 1940 Burnett published Salinger's first story, "The Young Folks," in *Story* magazine. It was followed by two more stories in 1942 and 1944. Burnett was fond of Salinger not only because he recognized his talent but probably also because both of them had lived in Vienna and both had come to love that city. He corresponded with Salinger throughout the year that Salinger served with the Army in Europe. Much of that correspondence has to do with Burnett's hope to publish a collection of Salinger's stories. But Salinger was already preoccupied with turning six stories about a boy named Holden Caulfield into a novel. That project developed into *The Catcher in the Rye*.

Burnett must have liked Salinger's later Vienna story, "A Girl I Knew" (1948), especially because the central character is nineteen-year-old Salinger in disguise. And Burnett must have been as amused as most of the story's readers about the fellow's fantasy of flying a plane with a silent engine to Austria and bombing the Nazis.

Because Salinger expressed no concern about the Nazis when he returned from Vienna in 1938, it is likely that he did not entertain his revenge fantasy until he wrote "A Girl I Knew" ten years later. After all, he did not mention the Nazis in his column for the *Ursinus Weekly* or in conversations with classmates. If he had, someone at Ursinus would have mentioned it. It therefore seems that unlike his alter ego, John, in "A Girl I Knew" Salinger did not read the *New York Times* stories about the Nazis' brutal treatment of the Austrian Jews when he returned from Vienna.

Why this unconcern? One explanation is that Salinger was a typical nineteen-year-old and less interested in politics than in "winning high honors in beer hoisting," as a contributor's note for one of his early stories puts it. Another reason for young Salinger's unconcern about the Nazis probably had to do with his upbringing and his parents' deliberate downplaying of the family's Jewishness. Since Salinger did not identify with the Austrian Jews, he was not interested in what the Nazis were doing to them.

3

Continued Unconcern
about the Nazis

Salinger's lack of concern about the Nazis continued after Hitler started World War II in September 1939, after the Wehrmacht marched into Paris in June 1940, after they invaded Soviet Russia in June 1941, and even after Salinger joined the army in April 1942. Throughout those years he did not seem to be interested in the war in Europe, even after it became widely known that the Nazis had begun to systematically murder Jews in mass executions.

In 1941, when Salinger published the first of three stories about young men in the US Army, he did not mention the Nazis and the war in Europe; nor did he do so in his next two stories, published in 1942 and 1944. In fact, he did not mention the Nazis in his military stories until after he found out that he was going to be part of the US Army's war effort in Europe.

Salinger's early unconcern about the Nazis and the war in Europe is not so strange when we realize that most of the population in the United States didn't care either. Despite the Nazis' invasion of Poland, and despite France and England's declarations of war on Germany, most Americans wanted the United States to stay out of the war in Europe. And so President Roosevelt was re-elected in 1940 on the promise of keeping the United States out of the war. It was not until the Japanese attack on Pearl Harbor on December 7, 1941, and Germany and Italy's declaration of war on the United States on December 11, 1941, that more Americans began to take an interest in the war in Europe.

Salinger's continued unconcern about the Nazis and the European war can be explained in terms of three distractions: his ambition to make a name for himself as a writer, the Japanese attack on Pearl Harbor, and his hope of receiving a commission as an officer in the army. These distractions left their marks in the military stories he wrote between 1941 and 1943.

The Wehrmacht's victory parade through Paris (German Bundesarchiv)

Salinger's first military story, "The Hang of It," was published in 1941, over a year after the German army had marched into Paris. Nevertheless, Salinger does not mention the war in Europe in the story. This is odd because Salinger had spent ten months in Austria and Poland, and one would think he might make at least a passing reference to the German war machine rolling over Poland, France, and other European countries. Instead Salinger offers a description of basic military training that makes no reference to war and is so upbeat that the US Army used it as recruitment propaganda. It was reprinted it in the 1942 *Kit Book for Soldiers, Sailors, and Marines*, which was given to all new recruits.

The reason Salinger did not put "The Hang of It" in the context of the Nazis' conquest of Europe can be explained in part as a result of his ambition to make a name for himself as a writer. The first step in his quest to achieve recognition was to break into the glamorous magazine market. As he shows in his September 1941 *Esquire* piece, "The Heart of a Broken Story," he carefully studied what kinds of stories would sell, and it was upbeat stories that sold. Mentioning the war in Europe and the Nazis would not be upbeat.

"The Hang of It" appeared in *Collier's* magazine on July 12, 1941. At that time, American magazines often published stories about young men in the army, and "The Hang of It" is such a piece of formula fiction. *Collier's* billed it as "A Short Short Story Complete on This Page."[1]

As the story begins, the anonymous narrator observes army recruits being drilled. He notices a young man by the name of Harry who is spectacularly incompetent, and he says that this young man reminds him of a clumsy recruit named Bobby Pettit who went through basic training back in World War I.

The narrator then tells the story of this Bobby Pettit, whom his drill sergeant called "the dumbest . . . the stoopidest . . . the clumsiest gink I ever seen." Whenever Sergeant Grogan yelled at Bobby because Bobby ported arms instead presenting arms, because he did not make up his pack correctly, or because he failed to pitch his tent so it would stay up, Bobby's reply to the sergeant was, "I'll get the hang of it." And despite the sergeant's harassment, Bobby said, "I like the Army. Some day I'll be a colonel or something."

In the surprise ending of the story, the narrator and his wife watch the new recruits during their first parade. In this parade, young Harry stands out because he is often out of step and because he drops his rifle while the national anthem is being played. After the parade, Sergeant Grogan comes to greet the narrator, and it turns out that the narrator is Colonel Bobby Pettit and that the clumsy recruit is his son, Harry.

What is unusual about "The Hang of It" is that it is so cheerful and so oblivious to the reality of war. The recruits do not come across as soldiers who are being trained to kill enemies but as boy scouts who are being trained to march in parades. But this is the kind of story that sold in early 1941. Even if Salinger had been concerned about the Nazis imposing their rule on the rest of Europe, he apparently realized that the public did not want to hear about it. And his own career as a writer depended on writing stories that gave the public what they wanted, not what they should be concerned about.

The second distraction that kept Salinger from writing about the Nazis was the Japanese attack on Pearl Harbor on December 7, 1941. After Salinger had completely ignored the war in his first military story, the Japanese attack on Pearl Harbor came as a wake-up call. Four days after the attack, Salinger wrote to his mentor Whit Burnett and referred to "the sneaky bombing last Sunday." He also reported that he immediately went to enlist in the army, but because of a heart ailment he was "classified I-B with all the other cripples and faggets [*sic*]."[2] He was later reclassified and started basic training at Fort Dix, New Jersey, on April 27, 1942.

Illustration from Salinger's
"The Hang of It" (*Collier's*)

The fact that Salinger wanted to enlist in the army the week after Pearl Harbor forecasts the patriotic attitude of the characters in his two stories "Personal Notes of an Infantryman" and "Soft-Boiled Sergeant." But while these two stories mention the Japanese attack on Pearl Harbor, they do not mention the Nazis or the war in Europe.

"Personal Notes of an Infantryman" appeared in *Collier's* magazine on December 12, 1942, and it is another "Short Short Story Complete on this

Page."[3] Like "The Hang of It," this story also has a surprise ending that reveals the identity of the narrator. And like "The Hang of It," it does not mention the Nazis or the war in Europe. But this time that is understandable because the public would be more interested in stories that supported the war effort against the Japanese than stories about the war in Europe, which did not yet involve the United States.

"Personal Notes" is told by a young officer who is serving on an army base where new recruits receive basic training. One day, a middle-aged man named Lawlor shows up in this lieutenant's orderly room and wants to enlist in the army. The narrator looks through the man's papers and tells him: "You are a technical foreman in a key war industry. . . . Have you stopped to consider that a man your age might be of greatest service to his country if he just stuck to his job?" Next, the young officer asks Lawlor how his wife and his two sons feel about his decision to go to war. Lawlor's reply is that his wife is "delighted." He adds: "Don't you know all wives are anxious to see their husbands go to war." Then he says that one of his sons is in the army and the other was in the navy "until he lost an arm at Pearl Harbor." What happened to his second son turns out to be Lawlor's motivation for enlisting. This becomes clear after Lawlor has completed basic training, and his commanding officer drops him from the list of soldiers to be shipped to the Pacific. Lawlor complains, saying, "*I want action.*"

After Lawlor is promoted first to corporal and then to sergeant, he finally gets his wish and prepares to ship out and fight the Japanese. In the story's last paragraph, the narrator mentions that he and his brother Pete went to see Lawlor off at the boat, and he reveals that Lawlor is his father.

This story is quite different from "The Hang of It," not only because of the important role played by Pete Lawlor's loss of his arm but also because Salinger now deals with the kind of propaganda that the government and the media employed to promote enlistments in the military. When Lawlor says that "all wives are anxious to see their husbands go to war," Salinger underlines the falseness of that statement by telling us that Lawlor made the comment while "smiling peculiarly." Later in the story, there is a similar criticism of the clichés of war propaganda when the narrator says that he wanted to console Lawlor's wife (who is his mother) about Lawlor going to war by "alluding to Lawlor as being one of our gallant boys now." The narrator rejects that idea not only because his mother already knows that her husband is gallant but also because "the allusion was labored and phony."

This is the first time that Salinger used the word *phony* in his published fiction. That term becomes Holden Caulfield's favorite word of condemnation in *The Catcher in the Rye*, but it does not appear in the early Holden Caulfield stories "I'm Crazy" (1945) and "Slight Rebellion off Madison" (1946).

"Soft-Boiled Sergeant" is another story that shows why Pearl Harbor distracted Salinger's attention from the Nazis. It was originally titled "Death of a Dogface," but the story's title was changed by the editors of the *Saturday Evening Post* before it was published on April 15, 1944. Although this story is essentially war propaganda, Salinger also criticizes the way war movies depict the deaths of soldiers.

The narrator of "Soft-Boiled Sergeant" is a GI named Philly Burns who complains that his wife always makes him take her to see war movies. He dislikes war movies because:

> You see a lot of real handsome guys always getting shot pretty neat, right where it don't spoil their looks none, and they always got plenty of time, before they croak, to give their love to some doll back home. . . . Then you don't see no more, except you hear some guy with a bugle handy take time off to blow taps. Then you see the dead guy's home town, and around a million people, including the mayor and the dead guy's folks and his doll, and maybe the President, all around the guy's box, making speeches and wearing medals.[4]

Then Philly Burns begins his story of Sergeant Burke, who took him under his wing when he, Philly, joined the army as a homeless young boy. As it turns out, Burke sympathized with Philly because Burke himself had joined the army at a young age when he got tired of being a hobo riding freight cars. Burke was an excellent soldier in World War I and came out of that war with a large number of medals, including the French Croix de Guerre. When young Philly had a crying jag in the barracks because he felt so lonely and because the other soldiers made fun of him, Sergeant Burke let the boy wear all of his medals under his tunic. This kind gesture made the other soldiers accept Philly despite his extreme youth.

A few years later, Philly hears from an acquaintance how Sergeant Burke died during the Japanese attack on Pearl Harbor. While trying to save the lives of three young recruits, Burke was hit by machine gun fire from a Japanese plane. The report was that Burke died with "four holes between his shoulders," and "half of his jaw was shot off." Philly concludes: "He died all by himself and he didn't leave no messages to give to no girl or nobody, and there wasn't nobody throwing a big classy funeral for him here in the States, and no hot-shot bugler blowed taps for him."

Salinger later came to hate the army, but the stories "Personal Notes of an Infantryman" and "Soft-Boiled Sergeant" both depict the army as a nurturing institution peopled by officers and sergeants who are kind and humane. Salinger best expresses his attitude toward the army in "Soft-Boiled Sergeant" when he makes Philly Burns say, "I met more good guys in the army than I ever knowed when I was a civilian."

Another story that reflects Salinger's initial positive attitude toward the army is "This Sandwich Has No Mayonnaise." He must have written it at about the same time as "Personal Notes of an Infantryman" and "Soft-Boiled Sergeant." Like "Personal Notes," "This Sandwich" depicts an army lieutenant as a good guy while the later stories show army officers to be unlikeable. But the story was not published in *Esquire* magazine until October 1945, when Salinger's attitude toward the army had already turned negative.

"This Sandwich Has No Mayonnaise" is one of two wartime stories that take place on an unnamed Army Air Corps base in Georgia (the other story is "Two Lonely Men"). Here Salinger draws on his service at a base in Bainbridge, Georgia. In his biography of Salinger, Kenneth Slawenski claims that even though Salinger was not "mechanically inclined," he taught Army Air Corps cadets "the workings of an airplane" and "spent his days instructing recruits and training pilots."[5] In fact, Salinger's job at Bainbridge had nothing to do with airplanes. Instead, "he corrected papers in a ground school for aviation cadets," as William Maxwell explains in a biographical sketch that Salinger himself vetted as publicity for *The Catcher in the Rye*.[6]

"This Sandwich Has No Mayonnaise" is the story of Sergeant Vincent Caulfield, whose younger brother Holden is missing in action in the Pacific. (Salinger made Holden the central character in *The Catcher in the Rye*, and he describes Vincent's death in the story "The Stranger.") The gist of "This Sandwich" is that Vincent has been ordered to chaperone thirty GIs to a dance in town. He accidentally lets three extra GI's get on the truck that will take them to Miz Jackson's dance hall, and he is able to convince only two of the three extra men to stand down. One soldier adamantly demands to be taken to the dance because he was one of the first to sign up for it. A young lieutenant from Special Services solves the problem by calling his own sister and badgering her into coming to the dance so the stubborn extra GI does not miss out.

Throughout his ordeal of trying to get three GI's off the truck, Vincent is distracted by the news that his brother Holden is missing in action. He thinks, "Where are you Holden? Never mind the Missing stuff. Stop playing around. Show up somewhere."[7]

So, like "Personal Notes of an Infantryman" and "Soft-Boiled Sergeant," "This Sandwich Has No Mayonnaise" acknowledges the war with the Japanese but not the war with the Germans. One reason for Salinger's unconcern about the Nazis in these stories may have been that the Japanese had already killed

American soldiers in large numbers, while the Wehrmacht did not yet pose a threat to Americans.

It is more difficult to understand why Salinger does not mention the Nazis in any of his later Glass Family stories, even though four of the Glass siblings served in the armed forces during World War II. In "Uncle Wiggily in Connecticut" (1948), Eloise Wengler mentions that her former lover Walt Glass died in a freak accident while serving with the US Army of Occupation in Japan. In "Raise High the Roof Beam, Carpenters" (1955), we find that Boo Boo (Beatrice) was serving in the navy and that Buddy was stationed on an army base in Georgia. And in "Seymour: An Introduction" (1959), we learn that Seymour had a desk job on an Army Air Force base in California and that he and Buddy later served in Europe, ending up with the US Army of Occupation in Germany. Still, no one in the Glass family ever mentions the Nazis, and in "A Perfect Day for Bananafish" Seymour Glass even sends his wife a book of German poems and suggests she should learn German to appreciate them.

A third reason Salinger was distracted from paying attention to the Nazis and the war in Europe was his ambition to become an officer. His unpublished letters at the Copyright Department of the National Archives show that he applied twice to be admitted to officer candidate school and was rejected both times. He expressed his frustration in a 1943 letter to Whit Burnett in which he wrote: "I want to be an officer so bad, and they just won't let me."[8]

After the second rejection, Salinger's attitude toward the army took a sour grapes turn. This is reflected in two stories, "Once a Week Won't Kill You," published in the November/December 1944 issue of *Story* magazine, and in the unpublished story "Two Lonely Men."

Salinger's disappointment at being denied the opportunity to attend officer candidate school can explain why the story "Once a Week Won't Kill You" celebrates Dickie Camson's choice to serve as a common soldier even though he has the qualifications to be an officer.

The story takes place in March 1944, and there are only three characters in it, Dickie Camson, his wife, Virginia, and his Aunt Rena. Dickie has not tried to shirk military service even though his parents are extremely wealthy. In the first half of the story Dickie is talking to Virginia about what he expects her to do while he is gone, and in the second part of the story he tells his Aunt Rena that he is about to leave for the army.

During the first conversation, we find out that Dickie's unwillingness to apply for officer candidate school is a sore subject between him and his status-conscious wife. While Dickie is packing his suitcase to leave for basic training,

Virginia asks him to phone a colonel they know who is in the Counter Intelligence Corps because he may still be able to pull some strings for him. She says: "I mean *you speak French and German and all*. He'd certainly *get you at least a commission*. I mean you know how *miserable* you'll be just being a private or something. I mean you even hate to *talk* to people and everything."[9] But Dickie doesn't want to discuss "that commission business," and Virginia responds by saying, "Well, I hope at *least* they send you to *London*. I mean where there's some *civilized* people." It doesn't occur to Virginia that Dickie might wind up in the trenches fighting the Wehrmacht.

At the end of the conversation, Dickie asks Virginia to take care of his Aunt Rena while he is gone and to take her to the movies at least once a week. Knowing that Virginia isn't as fond of his aunt as he is, he tells her, "once a week won't kill you."

When Dickie goes to see Aunt Rena to tell her that he expects to be shipped abroad to fight in Europe, we find out that Rena lost her mind when her fiancé died in the First World War. This becomes clear when she gives Dickie a letter of recommendation to her dead fiancé, second lieutenant Tom Cleve, saying, "He'll look after you till you get settled and all." It is significant that Aunt Rena's fiancé was a second lieutenant. That is the rank Dickie Camson and J. D. Salinger would have been given upon graduation from officer candidate school. Both were actually better off not getting a commission because in the infantry, second lieutenants were platoon leaders and accounted for a disproportionate number of casualties in both European wars.

Salinger portrays Dickie Camson's willingness to go to war in the ranks of the common soldiers as admirable, but the story never mentions why Dickie is willing to risk getting killed. Above all, the story never mentions the Germans that he will be fighting in Europe.

Likewise, there is no mention of the Nazis in the unpublished story "Two Lonely Men."[10] This story also takes place on an Army Air Corps base in Georgia, as does "This Sandwich Has No Mayonnaise." The two lonely men of the title are a sergeant by the name of Maydee and a captain by the name of Huggins. Salinger describes Sergeant Maydee as tough and competent and his boss Captain Huggins as incompetent and ignorant. Huggins was a pharmacist in civilian life, and because of his college degree, he was given a commission when he was drafted into the Army Air Corps. He has no understanding whatsoever of aircraft or navigation, but he was made commanding officer of a pilot training school. The story oozes with Salinger's disdain for officers like Captain Huggins.

"Two Lonely Men" is about the failed friendship between Sergeant Maydee and Captain Huggins, and it subverts the theme of the special friendship among soldiers that Salinger had developed earlier in "Soft-Boiled Sergeant." Officers like Huggins and noncommissioned officers like Maydee usually don't socialize, but these two often play cards and drink scotch together. When Maydee learns that Huggins's wife is having an affair with a pilot trainee, Maydee promises to save Huggins's marriage and goes to see the wayward wife. After his heart-to-heart talk with the wife, Maydee is invited to dinner by the Hugginses, and it looks as though Maydee has managed to save their marriage.

But at the end of the story Maydee requests to be sent to the Pacific for combat duty and makes disparaging comments about his "friend" Huggins. This suggests that Maydee has been sleeping with Huggins's wife. So in this story Salinger seems to be questioning his earlier notion that the army welds soldiers together in friendships stronger than those in civilian life. It is Salinger's first story that is critical of the US Army, but like Salinger's previous military stories, "Two Lonely Men" also avoids mentioning the Nazis and the war in Europe.

In December 1942, while Salinger was stationed at the Army Air Corps base in Georgia, an event occurred that should have made him pay attention to the Nazis but didn't. That event was a declaration by the governments of the United States, the United Kingdom, and nine Allied countries concerning what the Nazis called "the Final Solution of the Jewish Problem."

There had been massacres of Jews after the Wehrmacht overran Poland in September 1939, but the systematic extermination of Jews did not begin until June 1941 after the invasion of Soviet Russia. As early as August 1941, in a BBC radio broadcast, British prime minister Winston Churchill mentioned mass shootings of Jews in Poland and Russia. Then in May 1942, the Polish government-in-exile in London published a pamphlet titled *The Extermination of Jews in Occupied Poland*. By that time, the Nazis were no longer murdering Jews by shooting them but were transporting them to extermination camps and gassing them at the rate of up to five thousand a day. This became known to the Allies by the end of 1942. And on December 17, 1942, the British and American governments and their allies issued the *Joint Declaration by Members of the United Nations*. It documents the beginning of what we now call the Holocaust.

The declaration reports that the Nazis "are now carrying into effect Hitler's oft repeated intention to exterminate the Jewish people of Europe." Then it mentions the monstrous scope of those mass murders:

> From all the occupied countries Jews are being transported in conditions
> of appalling horror and brutality to Eastern Europe. In Poland, which has

been made the principal Nazi slaughterhouse, the ghettos established by
the German invader are being systematically emptied of all Jews except a
few highly skilled workers required for war industries. None of those taken
away are ever heard of again. The able-bodied are slowly worked to death
in labor camps. The infirm are left to die of exposure and starvation or are
deliberately massacred in mass executions. The number of victims of these
bloody cruelties is reckoned in many hundreds of thousands of entirely
innocent men, women, and children.[11]

The declaration ends with the United States, the United Kingdom, and
their allies condemning "in the strongest possible terms this bestial policy of
cold-blooded extermination" and declaring "their solemn resolution to insure
that those responsible for these crimes shall not escape retribution." The British
foreign secretary Sir Anthony Eden read this declaration to the British House
of Commons, and it was published both by the London *Times* and the *New York
Times*.

The *New York Times* reprinted the declaration on its front page on December
18, 1942. The headline read, "11 Allies Condemn Nazi War on Jews." I cannot
imagine that Salinger missed the article. Since he was raised in New York City,
we can assume that he kept reading the *New York Times*. And because he came
from a Jewish family and had spent some time in Austria and Poland in his
youth, he should have been interested in the genocide the Nazis were embarked
on in Europe. However, he did not refer to the Nazis in his fiction until over a
year later, and he never acknowledged the Holocaust but only briefly referred
to one specific concentration camp in a story that appeared three years after
the end of the war.

It is odd that Salinger never mentions the Nazis and the war in Europe in the
military stories he wrote between 1941 and 1944 or in his letters from that time
period. But this unconcern about the Nazis can be explained in terms of his intense focus on his career as a writer, the Japanese attack on Pearl Harbor, and
his dashed hope to be admitted to officer candidate school. Of these three distractions, his ambition to become a first-rate writer remains the overarching
one throughout his service with the US Army in Europe. As I will show in a
later chapter, Salinger's single-minded focus on his writing career is revealed in
a letter he wrote during the bloody Battle of the Hürtgen Forest. In that letter
he went on and on about literary matters and completely blocked out the war
and the Nazis while the Wehrmacht was killing the soldiers of his Twelfth
Infantry Regiment by the hundreds.

4

Ready to Kill Nazis

After Salinger had worked desk jobs at army bases in Georgia and Ohio for over a year and had his application to officer candidate school turned down twice, the army finally recognized that he could be of best value to the war effort as a Counter Intelligence Corps (CIC) agent. Not only did he speak French and German, he had also spent some time in Austria and Poland. But in order to be accepted into the Counter Intelligence Corps, Salinger had to agree to a demotion from staff sergeant to corporal. (By the time he was discharged from the army in November 1945, he had regained his previous rank.) Salinger agreed to the transfer, and in October 1943 he was sent to the Counter Intelligence School at Fort Holabird, Maryland, where he began his training for the work he was to do after the invasion of Nazi-occupied Europe. Now he could no longer avoid thinking and writing about the Nazis.

It must have been during his time at Fort Holabird that Salinger wrote "Last Day of the Last Furlough," the story in which he mentions the Nazis for the first time. But "Last Day" was not published in the *Saturday Evening Post* until July 15, 1944, a month after D-Day.

In "Last Day," Salinger reveals mixed feelings about the war. On the one hand, he deplores war propaganda and the tendency of veterans to glorify war; on the other hand, he celebrates the specialness of friendships among soldiers. In addition, Salinger indulges in a bit of fear mongering when his central character imagines the enemies of the United States invading the country and threatening his family. These thoughts lead him to declare his willingness to kill "Nazis and Fascists and Japs," which makes the story read almost like war propaganda. In none of his later stories does Salinger express feelings as patriotic and anti-Nazi as those in "Last Day of the Last Furlough."

American propaganda cartoon: Hitler, Mussolini, Hirohito (National Archives)

"Last Day of the Last Furlough" marks the first appearance in Salinger's fiction of Sergeant John F. Gladwaller Jr., nicknamed "Babe" (Gladwaller also appears in "A Boy in France" and in "The Stranger"). He has the same military ID number as Jerome D. Salinger, ASN 32325200. And in "The Stranger" we find out that Gladwaller also served in Salinger's Twelfth Infantry Regiment. But unlike Salinger, he was a combat soldier and not a CIC agent.

"Last Day" takes place on the day before Gladwaller and his friend Vincent Caulfield are scheduled to return to their army unit, which is about to be shipped out for combat in Europe. During the Gladwallers' family dinner with their guest Vincent, Babe talks at length about the war and the Nazis, and he makes three statements about Hitler.

Babe makes his first Hitler comment after his father recounts his experiences of fighting in World War I. This sets Babe off on a diatribe against the veterans of his father's generation who glorify war "as if it had been some kind of rugged, sordid game by which the society of your day weeded out the men from the boys." Babe believes the men of his father's generation think themselves "a little superior" for having fought in World War I, and so do the Germans who fought in that war. Then Babe says, "When Hitler provoked this one, the younger generation in Germany were ready to prove themselves as good or better than their fathers."[1] In this comment Salinger reveals an astonishing misconception. When he makes Babe Gladwaller say that Hitler provoked World War II, he suggests that the Nazis did not actually start World War II by invading Poland, but that Hitler goaded some other country into starting the war.

In his second Hitler statement, Babe talks about how to make sure there will be no "future Hitlers" after World War II. He gets around to that idea after he says "it's the moral duty of those who fight and have fought in this war to keep our mouths shut, once it's over, never again to mention it in any way." And then he argues that if the American, British, French, Japanese, and German soldiers all come back "talking, writing, painting, making movies of heroism and cockroaches and foxholes and blood, then future generations will always be doomed to future Hitlers." This comment suggests that Salinger saw Hitler merely as a power-hungry warmonger, and that he did not know—or did not want to know—that the Nazis were in the process of implementing Hitler's plans for the extermination of the entire Jewish population of Europe.

Babe's concluding remarks about Hitler are a joke about Hitler's ego and don't acknowledge him as a genocidal megalomaniac. Babe says: "It's never occurred to boys to have contempt for wars, to point to soldiers' pictures in history books, laughing at them. If German boys had learned to be contemptuous of violence, Hitler would have had to take up knitting to keep his ego warm." So Babe's speech is really more concerned about war in general than about Hitler and the Nazis.

In contrast to this antiwar speech are two passages in the story where Babe and Vincent are discussing their feelings about the army and the war. Vincent and Babe believe that they are very different from civilians. Vincent says: "GIs—especially GIs who are friends—belong together these days. It's no good being with civilians any more. They don't know what we know and we're no longer used to what they know." Babe agrees: "I never really knew anything about friendship before I was in the Army." This passage echoes a statement by the narrator of the earlier story "Soft-Boiled Sergeant," who says: "I met more good guys in the Army than I ever knowed when I was a civilian."[2] These are the two most positive statements Salinger made about the army in all of his fiction, and ironically they sound a lot like the kind of war propaganda Babe castigates in his speech at the dinner table.

Two other passages in "Last Day" also have the ring of war propaganda. In both passages Babe and Vincent express their willingness to kill enemy soldiers. Vincent has been eager to kill ever since he received word that his brother Holden had gone missing and had probably died while fighting the Japanese somewhere in the Pacific. He tells Babe: "I want to kill so badly I can't sit still. Isn't that funny? All my life I've even avoided fistfights, always getting out of them by talking fast. Now I want to shoot it out with people."

Less eager to kill than Vincent, Babe explains that he believes in World War II because if he didn't, he would have gone to a conscientious objectors' camp for the duration of the war: "I believe in killing Nazis and Fascists and Japs, because there is no other way that I know of."[3] Why Babe feels this way becomes clear in the final scene of the story, when he goes to check on his sleeping kid sister Mattie. He thinks to himself, "*No enemy is banging on our door, waking her up. But it could happen if I don't go out and meet him with my gun. And I will, and I'll kill him.*"

This scene might have been inspired by the Norman Rockwell painting *Freedom from Fear*, published in the *Saturday Evening Post* a year earlier on March 13, 1943. In that picture a couple looks in on their sleeping children, and the newspaper the father holds in his hand has a headline starting with the words "Bombings kill." I am sure Salinger saw that picture because "Last Day of the Last Furlough" was also published in the *Saturday Evening Post*, and so were four other Salinger stories.

Babe's internal monologue about wanting to protect his young sister seems a bit far-fetched because in 1943 when Salinger wrote the story, neither the Germans nor the Italians nor the Japanese had the capacity to invade or even bomb the United States. Here Salinger is going out on a limb to make Babe into an icon representing the hundreds of thousands that were being sent to fight in Europe and in the Pacific.

"Last Day of the Last Furlough" stands out in Salinger's fiction because it contains his only explicit anti-Nazi statement and his most positive statements about the US Army. But the story also sends conflicting signals about Salinger's attitude toward the war. On the one hand, he condemns the glorification of soldiering. On the other hand, he himself glorifies those who are willing to fight for their country, and he celebrates the specialness of friendships among soldiers. And although Salinger has Gladwaller say that it is the "moral duty" of those fighting in World War II "to keep their mouths shut" about their experiences, Salinger did not keep his own mouth shut but wrote several stories that reflect events he experienced in the war.

5

The Slapton Sands Disasters

In January 1944, Corporal J. D. Salinger and some sixty other CIC personnel were sent to England to train for the invasion of Europe. At the British Military Intelligence School in Tiverton, Devon, they received instruction on how to collect information from abandoned German command posts, how to interrogate Wehrmacht prisoners and French collaborators, and how to track down Nazi spies. Because the Fourth Infantry Division's CIC detachment was scheduled to land with the first assault troops, Salinger and his fellow CIC agents had to participate in four landing exercises. These landings occurred at a stretch of the English coastline near Slapton Sands that happens to look a lot like the Utah Beach sector of the Normandy coast, where the Fourth Division was scheduled to go ashore on D-Day. Salinger did not comment on those practice landings, but he did mention his counterintelligence training for the D-Day invasion in part one of the story "For Esmé—With Love and Squalor."

The Slapton Sands landing exercises were top secret, and participating troops were quarantined until D-Day. Also Salinger's CIC detachment had the job of keeping the lid on two major military disasters that occurred during one of the landings, the one code-named Exercise Tiger.

Exercise Tiger took place on April 27 and 28, 1944, and involved thirty thousand troops. By the time the exercise was over, more than one hundred soldiers had been killed by friendly fire from a British warship, and more than six hundred soldiers and sailors had been killed when German torpedo boats sank two large landing ships and crippled a third. These tragedies were due to shoddy planning on the part of the army and navy leadership, to an unwise decision by the admiral in charge, and to a lack of communication between the British navy and the American troops.[1]

To understand why the twin disasters happened, it is necessary to know what the plan for Exercise Tiger was. Below I have reprinted the orders for Exercise Tiger that were issued by General Dwight D. Eisenhower, the supreme commander of all forces that were to participate in the D-Day landings. These orders were slightly modified during the days preceding the landing. But one of their essential features, the use of live ammunition in the bombardment of the beach by navy vessels, remained unchanged.

Supreme Headquarters
Allied Expeditionary Force
G-3 Division

19 April 1944

Subject: Exercise Tiger

1. Exercise Tiger will involve the concentration, marshalling and embarkation of troops in the Torbay-Plymouth area, and a short movement by sea under the control of the US Navy, disembarkation with Naval and Air support at Slapton Sands, a beach assault using [live] service ammunition, the securing of a beachhead and a rapid advance inland.

2. Major troop units are the VII Corps Troops, 4th Infantry Division, the 101st and 52nd Airborne Divisions, 1st Engineer Special Brigade, Force 'U' and supporting Air Force units.

3. During the period H-60 to H-45 minutes, fighter-bombers attack inland targets on call from the 101st AB Division and medium bombers attack three targets along the beach. Additional targets will be bombed by both fighter-bombers and medium bombers on call from ground units. Simulated missions will also be flown with the target areas marked by smoke pots.

4. Naval vessels fire upon beach obstacles from H-50 to H-Hour. Smoke may be used during the latter part of the bombardment both from naval craft by 4.2 chemical mortars and at H-Hour by planes, if weather conditions are favourable. Naval fire ceases at H-Hour.

5. The schedule of the exercise is as follows:
    22 April—Move to marshalling area commences.
    D-Day 27 April—101st AB Div simulates landing. Preparatory bombardment by air and Navy. Assault landing and advance of the 4th Div.

28–29 April—Advance of 4th Div. & 101st AB Div. continues. 82nd
AB Div. simulates landing, secures and holds objective.
(Exercise terminates on 29 April)
TOP SECRET[2]

As these orders show, Exercise Tiger was intended to be an almost full-scale practice landing. "Almost" because due to a shortage of aircraft, the airborne units (paratroopers) were not flown in but brought in on trucks. The troops that participated in the exercise were the very units that landed at Utah Beach in Normandy less than two months later.

The first disaster occurred during the shelling of the beach by the British heavy cruiser HMS *Hawkins* while American troops were landing. This friendly fire incident happened because of a last-minute decision to postpone the start of the landings by one hour. A contributing factor was that the printed orders mistakenly assigned different radio frequencies to the British warships and the American landing craft. As a result the landing craft did not find out about the change in their orders.

H-Hour—the time the troops were to land—was originally set to be 7:30. The *Hawkins* was scheduled to shell the beach from 6:40 to 7:30. But because a number of landing craft were slow to approach the shore, Rear Admiral Donald P. Moon decided to delay H-Hour to 8:30. This meant that the bombardment of the beach by the *Hawkins* was now to commence at 7:40.

Admiral Moon was unaware that because of the different radio frequencies the skippers of the landing craft could not receive the message he sent. Thus the first two assault waves landed as originally planned. Salinger's CIC detachment went ashore at 7:30 with the first assault team. The second assault team landed shortly thereafter and was on the beach at 7:40 when the HMS *Hawkins* began its bombardment. As soon as Admiral Moon found out, he ordered the *Hawkins* to stop firing. But the *Hawkins* did not get the order until she had fired some 120 rounds, killing over one hundred American soldiers of the Eighth Infantry Regiment and the First Engineer Brigade. Admiral Moon felt so guilty about having caused this disaster that he committed suicide less than three months later, on August 5, 1944.

Salinger and his CIC detachment narrowly escaped death, but they must have seen the soldiers of the second assault wave blown to bits by the naval bombardment of the beach. As if this weren't bad enough, they also witnessed an even greater tragedy later that night when German torpedo boats sank two landing ships and heavily damaged a third.

This happened half an hour after midnight when a convoy of eight large transport ships carrying tanks and their crews entered Lyme Bay, where Slapton

LST unloading a Sherman tank at Utah Beach (National Archives)

German torpedo boat (British Imperial War Museum)

Sands is located. These LSTs (Landing Ship Tanks) were 350 feet long and 50 feet wide, and each carried ten tanks or fifteen half-track vehicles. In addition, every LST transported six small LCAs (Landing Craft Assault), each of which could carry thirty-two troops.

The convoy of the eight LSTs was screened by a picket line of British warships out at sea. Nevertheless, nine German torpedo boats managed to slip through. The heavy radio traffic in the Lyme Bay area had alerted the Germans that something unusual was going on. This radio traffic must have been between the British ships because the LSTs observed absolute radio silence. When the British ships discovered that enemy torpedo boats had gotten into Lyme Bay, they radioed the LSTs to alert them. But the LSTs did not receive those warnings because of the wrong radio frequencies that had been assigned to them.

What also contributed to the disaster was that the American landing force was protected by only one warship, the corvette HMS *Azalea*. That ship was smaller than the LSTs it was supposed to protect. Also, because the *Azalea* was sailing ahead of the column that it was supposed to protect rather than following behind, she was unable to engage the enemy torpedo boats and prevent them from firing their torpedoes.

Because of these mistakes, the German torpedo boats were able to attack the convoy for an hour and a half and launch over a dozen torpedoes at it. They hit three of the LSTs, sinking two of them and severely damaging a third. The death toll was 198 sailors of the US Navy and 441 soldiers of Salinger's Fourth Infantry Division, more than twice the fatalities that the division later suffered during the D-Day landings.

After Salinger's CIC detachment narrowly escaped the accidental shelling of the American troops by the HMS *Hawkins* and witnessed the German torpedo boats' sinking of two landing ships, they were given the task of standing guard in the local hospitals where the wounded were being treated. The CIC agents were to make sure that the survivors did not talk about Exercise Tiger and give away the D-Day plans. Also, the doctors were ordered not to ask the wounded any questions.

It has been asserted that the US Army engaged in a cover-up of the Slapton Sands disasters. This is only partially true. Two months after the D-Day landings, on August 7, 1944, the US Armed Forces newspaper *Stars and Stripes* ran a story about Exercise Tiger. But that story mentions only the casualties inflicted by the German torpedo boats; it does not mention the casualties that resulted from the accidental shelling of the American troops by the HMS *Hawkins*.

The friendly fire debacle at Slapton Sands was not uncovered until forty-five years after the incident. In his book *Channel Firing*, the British researcher Nigel Lewis cites interviews with sailors from the HMS *Hawkins* who reported that "there were heavy casualties amongst the American lads who went ashore" and that the skipper of the *Hawkins* and his officers "were considerably shaken when they realized the enormity of the tragedy on shore."[3] Lewis also spoke with an American soldier who had been on the burial detail that placed over one hundred victims of the accidental shelling in a temporary mass grave near Slapton Sands. After D-Day these remains were reburied in France, and the dead soldiers of Exercise Tiger were listed as having died during the D-Day invasion.

The fatalities resulting from the accidental shelling of American troops at Slapton Sands by the HMS *Hawkins* were never officially acknowledged. As Lewis reports, the number of victims surfaced by chance. In an October 1987 letter from Deputy Assistant Defense Secretary William E. Hart to Senator Robert Dole, Hart addressed the rumor that the victims of the Slapton Sands exercise "are buried anonymously under concrete in a mass grave." To lay that rumor to rest, Hart wrote that "the 749 American victims were *temporarily* interred at Slapton Sands."[4] The figure of 749 that Hart mentions is at odds with the official Exercise Tiger death toll of 639 that the supreme headquarters of the Allied Expeditionary Force released in August 1945. So the difference of 110 must be the number of the friendly fire victims who were not acknowledged by the US Army.

Exercise Tiger turned out to be a more realistic introduction to the horrors of war than Salinger could have expected. After all, he and his CIC detachment might all have been wounded or killed if they had been part of the second assault wave and not the first. Having been spared in this close call must have seemed especially fortunate to Salinger when he witnessed the even more horrific carnage caused by the attack of the German torpedo boats on the LSTs. I suspect that Salinger later came to see that the casualties at Slapton Sands were unnecessary because they resulted from the incompetence of the military leadership.

Despite the double tragedy at Slapton Sands, Salinger's attitude seems to have been positive as he was getting ready for the D-Day invasion. According to Werner Kleeman, who served as one of the Fourth Division's German-speaking interpreters, Salinger took extraordinary care to make sure that his jeep would work when it was driven off the landing craft and onto the beach. In his book *From Dachau to D-Day*, Kleeman says about Salinger: "Every day, he used to waterproof his jeep so that it would function under water. He must have done a perfect job, because not only did the jeep's motor not die during the journey, but it landed safely on French soil, with Salinger able to drive it."[5]

Because the US Army maintained the utmost secrecy about the upcoming invasion and forbade its soldiers to write home, Salinger's only account of his experiences in England is the fictional one in the story "For Esmé—With Love and Squalor." This is a two-part story. The first part takes place in England before the D-Day invasion, and the second part takes place in Germany after the end of the war. In this chapter I am concerned only with the pre-invasion part of the story.

The central character and narrator in "For Esmé" is a thinly disguised version of Salinger himself. His name is Sergeant X, and like Salinger he is a short story writer and an agent of the CIC. As Sergeant X explains: "In April of 1944, I was among some sixty American enlisted men who took a rather specialized pre-Invasion training course, directed by British Intelligence, in Devon, England." The course lasted three weeks, after which Sergeant X and his whole group were sent to London, where they were to be "assigned to infantry and airborne divisions mustered for the D Day landings."[6]

In part one of "For Esmé" Salinger never mentions the Nazis or the Germans, even though Sergeant X is being trained for the invasion of Nazi-occupied Europe. Instead of anti-Nazi statements, this part of the story contains a number of negative statements about American GIs.

For instance, Sergeant X is annoyed by his noisy fellow soldiers because they are disturbing his writing by playing ping-pong "just an axe length away." Also, Sergeant X reports that a thirteen-year-old British girl named Esmé who befriends him at a tea shop says that most of the American soldiers she's seen "act like animals." As she explains: "They're forever punching one another about, and insulting everyone. . . . One of them threw an empty whiskey bottle through my aunt's window."[7]

Salinger's decision not to mention the Nazis in the first part of the story is most striking when young Esmé tells Sergeant X that her father was killed while fighting in the British Army. Esmé does not say who killed her father. She only says that he was "slain" in North Africa. This means he must have been killed by soldiers of General Erwin Rommel's Afrika Korps. We also learn that Esmé's mother died—apparently in a German air raid on a large English city—and that Esmé and her brother were "evacuated" to live with their aunt. But Esmé does not seem to be angry at the Germans. She refers to the hard life that the war has brought the British civilians merely as "a method of existence that is ridiculous to say the least."

The lack of any references to the Nazis in part one of "For Esmé" supports the structure of the story. The title stems from a conversation between Sergeant X and Esmé. When Esmé learns that the sergeant is a short story writer, she asks him to write a story expressly for her, and she stipulates that it must be about squalor because she is "extremely interested in squalor." Sergeant X suspects that Esmé does not know what the word squalor means, but he promises to write such a story for her. And as Salinger ends part one of the story and begins part two, he has his narrator Sergeant X tell us that the second part will be about squalor. This implies that the first part is about love, or rather about the affection that Esmé feels for Sergeant X. Esmé expresses that affection in a letter in which she tells Sergeant X she hopes he will come out of the war "with all your faculties intact." In part two of the story we find that Sergeant X did not come out of the war with his faculties intact. I will discuss part two in a later chapter.

Even though Salinger and his CIC detachment were trained for the invasion of Nazi-occupied France, he makes no reference in part one of "For Esmé" to the Germans that Sergeant X would be confronting on D-Day. This is hard to understand because shortly before the time when the pre-invasion action of "For Esmé" takes place, the Germans had killed over four hundred soldiers of Salinger's Fourth Infantry Division at Slapton Sands. But as I will show in subsequent chapters, Salinger later witnessed two additional deadly disasters caused by US military leadership, and he eventually came to feel more hostile toward the US Army than toward the Nazis.

6

Under Fire from the Wehrmacht

When Salinger began his training as a CIC agent at Fort Holabird in Maryland, he probably did not expect to come under enemy fire once he was deployed in Europe. This would be understandable because army manuals state that CIC agents are expected to do "rear echelon" work, well behind the front lines. But the training exercises at Slapton Sands made him realize that his CIC detachment would be one of the first US Army units to come under fire from the Germans on D-Day. And they did. Also, two weeks after D-Day, Salinger and his driver were almost killed in a German artillery barrage, and he seems to have narrowly escaped death on several other occasions as well— for instance, during one of his regular visits to his Twelfth Infantry Regiment's command post in the Hürtgen Forest when the area came under mortar attack.

Salinger worked his D-Day experience into the unpublished story "The Magic Foxhole," his experience of being shelled by the Germans into part two of "For Esmé—With Love and Squalor," and his Hürtgen Forest experience into the story "The Stranger."

It is generally known that Salinger participated in the D-Day landings at Utah Beach, but there is disagreement about when he went ashore. The confusion arose because Salinger was assigned to the Twelfth Regiment of the Fourth Infantry Division, and it was assumed that he landed with that regiment at 10:30 a.m. on June 6, 1944, four hours after the first assault.

But according to the US Army's *History of the Counter Intelligence Corps*, "The 4th CIC Detachment went in with the 4th Infantry Division when it stormed UTAH Beach at 0645."[1] This means that, as at Slapton Sands, Salinger went ashore with the first assault group of the Eighth Regiment.

Utah Beach under German artillery fire (National Archives)

The German Wehrmacht did not defend Utah Beach as fiercely as Omaha Beach, where American troops suffered over two thousand fatalities. On Utah Beach, the fatalities of the Fourth Division were 197, less than half of what they were during the practice landing at Slapton Sands.[2] The casualties were so light at Utah Beach because the Germans had deployed very few machine guns in widely spaced pillbox bunkers, and only one far-away artillery emplacement was shelling the beach. So Salinger's Fourth Infantry Division was not pinned down on Utah Beach as were the assault units at Omaha Beach. The Eighth Regiment's After Action Report shows that it took them less than an hour to clear the beach of German troops.

Still, the D-Day landing was traumatic for Salinger. It haunted him for many years. His daughter, Margaret, remembers her father mentioning D-Day on more than one occasion: "'I landed on D-Day, you know,' he'd say to me darkly, soldier to soldier as it were, as if I understood the implications, the unspoken."[3] And Margaret also describes her father remembering D-Day while watching a group of young men doing construction work on his new home in New Hampshire: "'All those big strong boys,' he said, 'always on the front line, always the first to be killed, wave after wave of them.'"[4] This comment suggests that Salinger watched the rest of his Fourth Division come ashore at Utah Beach after the German artillery had found the range on them.

In his telling of the landing on Utah Beach in the unpublished story "The Magic Foxhole," Salinger draws directly on his D-Day experience. That first part of the story is historically accurate. But the second part of the story deals with a battle a few days after the landing. That part is pure fiction because Salinger's CIC detachment was not involved in any battles after D-Day.

The events of "The Magic Foxhole" take place when the front has moved several miles inland. The narrator is a soldier named Garrity who was wounded during the landing but is now well enough to drive a jeep packed with jerry cans of gasoline from the beach to the front.

On one of his inland trips Garrity picks up a soldier whom he immediately identifies as a college man. When he finds out that this man "ain't going no further than Division," Garrity says: "Anybody in back of Battalion that's got a uniform on is in the Army. Any poor son of a bitch in front of Battalion is a soldier."[5]

Here Garrity refers to the command posts of the "Division" and the "Battalion." But these references make sense only if we understand that a World War II infantry division consisted of three regiments, and each regiment consisted of three battalions. And while the command post of an infantry division was usually located several miles behind the front, the command posts of the battalions were usually close enough to the fighting to get hit by enemy artillery and mortars.

So when Garrity says that "anybody in back of Battalion that's got a uniform on is in the Army," he means that such a person is not a real soldier like "the poor son of a bitch in front of Battalion," whose life is in constant jeopardy. Since Garrity's passenger is headed for the division command post, which is quite a ways farther from the front than the battalion command post, Garrity says, "You're in the Army then, eh, Mac?" Here Salinger is poking fun at the CIC desk jockeys who worked safe jobs at division headquarters far behind the front.

The autobiographical part of "The Magic Foxhole" is Garrity's description of what Utah Beach looked like when his company went ashore. He tells the hitchhiker, "There wasn't nothing on the beach but the dead boys of 'A' and 'B' Company, and some dead sailor boys, and a Chaplain that was crawling around looking for his glasses in the sand. He was the only thing that was moving, and eighty-eight [artillery] shells were breaking all around him, and there he was crawling around on his hands and knees, looking for his glasses. He got knocked off. . . . That's what the beach looked like when I come in."[6]

This account of the D-Day landing in "The Magic Foxhole" is strikingly similar to one by a survivor of the Eighth Regiment, Private Ray A. Mann:

> Our team rushed out of the craft and headed across the beach in small groups, just like that about 15 to 20 feet across the beach, shells started to fall. The first few landed in a group just ahead of me. Up to that point, I felt like this was almost like previous maneouvres [*sic*] in Florida, even Slapton Sands. But when I saw our wounded men agonizing in pain and heard them scream, I knew that we were playing for keeps. A second group of shells landed near my group and hit apparently our First Sergeant. Never saw him again. The company clerk was also hit. . . . I finally reached the seawall and the German pillbox and paused to get my bearings. Even in the short time between my landing and the time we got to the seawall, I was shocked by the number of men who were landing and the number of wounded that I saw spread out over the beach. I saw a chaplain here and there praying over dead men.[7]

The two passages are so similar that it might seem as though Salinger read Mann's account before he wrote "The Magic Foxhole." But Salinger wrote the story sometime in 1944, and the interview with Private Mann was not published until 2004.

In the non-autobiographical part of "The Magic Foxhole," Garrity explains how his friend Lewis Gardner wound up with a full-fledged case of what Garrity calls "Battle Fatigue." Gardner was a former lawyer, and he had his nervous collapse after a two-day battle with the Germans. Out of his company of 208 soldiers, only thirty-five survived. And for all those casualties, the company advanced only a couple thousand feet through a swamp that the soldiers called the "Widow Makers' Swamp."

In this part of the story, Salinger fictionalizes the Fourth Division's slog through an area the Germans had flooded to slow down the Americans. But the battle for the "Widow Makers' Swamp" is completely fictional because there was no resistance when the men of the Fourth Division waded through the submerged area. However, as Colonel Gerden Johnson reports in the *History of the Twelfth Regiment in World War II*, some of the men almost drowned: "Beneath the muddy waters lurked a criss-cross of irrigation ditches, some of them seven feet deep."[8]

The title, "The Magic Foxhole," refers to the story's quasisupernatural elements. Gardner told the narrator, Garrity, that several times when he sought shelter in a foxhole, he found it occupied by a young man in a strange-looking uniform with a helmet that had a radio receiver built into it. Gardner discovered that this young man's name was Earl and that he was his, Gardner's, as yet unborn son who was now fighting in a war of the future. Gardner wanted to kill his son-to-be because he believed that with that act he would be able to prevent the future war that his son would be fighting in. Of course, Gardner was only imagining all this because he had gone out of his mind due to the stress of battle.

After Gardner has his nervous collapse, he is evacuated to a field hospital on the beach. Garrity finds him standing in the sand, wearing GI pajamas, refusing to lie down on a stretcher and "holding on tight to some pole they got stuck in the sand." As I will show in a later chapter, the symptoms of Gardner's case of battle fatigue are quite different from those of Salinger's nervous breakdown.

Both the narrator's account of the landing and the part of "The Magic Foxhole" that describes the two-day battle are notable for their lack of rancor toward the enemies. Garrity calls the Germans "Krauts" and not Nazis, and he has a grudging respect for them. This comes out in the following passage: "The Krauts, they was in a forest, like. And they was dug in deep—you know the way Krauts dig in like they didn't want to get out of the ground till the Americans was out of Europe."[9]

Even when Garrity talks about Hitler, his comment is not hostile. This reference occurs in a conversation with his friend Gardner, who is convinced that America will fight another war in Europe and does not want his unborn son to fight in it. Gardner says, "I thought we come over here to finish up this war stuff for good." And Garrity responds, "Maybe something happened again. Maybe another guy like Hitler cropped up."[10]

The phrase "another guy like Hitler" is reminiscent of the phrase "future Hitlers" in "Last Day of the Last Furlough." It shows that even after D-Day, Salinger was still so uninformed about the Nazis that he thought of Hitler as a garden-variety dictator and apparently did not know—or did not want to know—what had been public knowledge for over a year, namely that the Nazis were systematically exterminating the Jewish population of Europe.

Salinger could not get "The Magic Foxhole" published in 1944, and I believe the reason was that in the battle that Gardner and Garrity fight, he exaggerates the casualties the US Army suffered after the D-Day landings. Moreover, the story does not make any patriotic anti-Nazi statements and does not depict the Germans as the bloodthirsty killers of the American propaganda movies. Instead the Germans come across as a disembodied natural force rather than as flesh-and-blood human beings.

And even though Salinger's portrayal of the US Army in "The Magic Foxhole" is not as full of praise as it was in "The Hang of It," "Soft-Boiled Sergeant," and "Last Day of the Last Furlough," it is not as negative as in "For Esmé—With Love and Squalor." In "The Magic Foxhole," the only implied criticism of the US Army is the question of whether the gain of a few thousand feet of territory justifies the enormous losses that Garrity and Gardner's company suffer.

Another post–D-Day story in which Salinger refers to the Germans without rancor is "A Boy in France." It appeared in the *Saturday Evening Post* in 1945, but Salinger probably wrote it sometime in the summer of 1944, about the time the events of the story take place. The central character is Babe Gladwaller from "The Last Day of the Last Furlough." Now we find him in Normandy.

The story begins after a "long, rotten afternoon" of combat that the story doesn't describe or even summarize. That evening, Babe's unit is digging foxholes to secure the advance they have made against the Germans. Babe is too tired to dig his own foxhole and looks for one dug by the Germans. When he sees "a foxhole, a German one, unmistakably vacated by some Kraut," he finds that another GI has already taken possession of it. Gladwaller is lucky though: "He saw another Kraut hole [and] looking into it, he saw a gray woolen Kraut blanket, half spread, half bunched on the damp floor of the hole. It was a terrible blanket on which a German had recently lain and bled and probably died."[11] After Gladwaller lifts out "the heavy, bloody, unlamented Kraut blanket," he throws it into a nearby hedgerow.

As in "The Magic Foxhole," Salinger does not use the term Nazis but calls the enemies "Krauts" or "Germans." He also makes Babe show sympathy for the German soldier who had died in the foxhole: he seems to regret that this man's death went as "unlamented" as his blanket.

In his wartime correspondence with his mentor Whit Burnett, Salinger also refers to the enemies not as Nazis but as Germans. And even though Salinger almost became a casualty of a German artillery barrage during that time—an incident that he worked into part two of "For Esmé—With Love and Squalor"—he shows no anger at the Germans. For instance, in a postcard to Burnett he wrote six days after D-Day, Salinger talks chiefly about a collection of stories that he is too busy to go on with because he is doing "mostly interesting work," and he says that the French civilians are "mostly delighted to be rid of the Germans."[12]

I am wondering about the repetition of the word *mostly* in that postcard because one of the hallmarks of Salinger's style is extreme economy. But the daily reports of Salinger's CIC detachment offer an explanation. They show that a great deal of the work Salinger and his fellow CIC agents had to do was to follow up on tips by French people denouncing French collaborators or other French people who had worked for the Nazi construction workforce called Organisation Todt. For instance in the daily CIC report for June 9, 1944, Salinger's boss, Lieutenant Oliver Appleton, writes: "The mayor of St. Mere-Eglise [*sic*] denounced two former Todt Organization workers namely, Ernest Polichon, from St. Martin; Roger Ruch, from Frankville. These civilians admitted being Todt Organization workers and were sent to the VII Corps Prisoner of War cage."[13] The frequency of such denunciations suggests that a lot of French people saw nothing wrong in cooperating with the Germans. Salinger may have interpreted this fact as meaning that the German occupation of France was not as tyrannical as described in American war propaganda. That might be why he suggests in the postcard to Burnett that most of the French— but not all—were glad to be rid of the Germans and that most of his work as a CIC agent—but not all of it—was interesting.

In contrast to the postcard, a letter that Salinger wrote to Burnett on June 28 does not require any between-the-lines reading. After discussing his plans for the "Caulfield novel," Salinger talks about the war: "I don't think I can write a pithy paragraph or two about the whole affair. I'm still scared. But I'll tell you this: you never saw six-feet-two of muscles and typewriter ribbon get out of a jeep and into a ditch as fast as this baby can. And I don't get out till they start bulldozing an airfield over me. No use in being fool-hardy, I say."[14] Salinger wrote this letter on the day that the last Wehrmacht troops surrendered in the seaport of Cherbourg.

A passage in the story "For Esmé—With Love and Squalor" suggests that Salinger's letter to Burnett refers to a specific incident that occurred some nine days earlier near the small town of Valognes, thirteen miles south of Cherbourg. In "For Esmé," Sergeant X's jeep driver reminisces: "Remember that time, I and you drove into Valognes, and we got shelled for about two goddam hours."[15]

According to Colonel Johnson's *History of the Twelfth Infantry Regiment in World War II*, the Wehrmacht was driven out of Valognes on June 19, and according to the June 20 report of Salinger's CIC detachment, his unit began its work in Valognes on that day. This means it was probably on June 18 or 19 that Corporal Salinger and his driver John Keenan barely escaped being killed by German artillery.

An artillery or mortar barrage is something that comes out of nowhere like a lightning strike, and one cannot consider it the same kind of personal attack as being shot at directly by an enemy soldier with a rifle or a machine gun. But surviving such a barrage would make most people angry at those who almost killed them. Yet Salinger's comments about this incident in his letter to Burnett and his treatment of it in the story "For Esmé—With Love and Squalor" do not reveal any resentment toward the Germans.

It is remarkable that in the stories "The Magic Foxhole" and "A Boy in France" Salinger's narrators call the Germans not Nazis but Krauts. Even more remarkable is that Garrity, in "The Magic Foxhole," has a grudging admiration for the Krauts and that the narrator of "A Boy in France" feels pity for the Kraut who died in the foxhole that Babe Gladwaller seeks shelter in. Also, in "For Esmé—With Love and Squalor," Sergeant X is not angry at the Germans even though he narrowly escaped being killed in one of their artillery barrages.

In short, all three stories reveal a radical change in Salinger's attitude toward the Nazis when compared to "Last Day of the Last Furlough." In that story, written a year before D-Day, the central character, Babe Gladwaller, says that he believes in killing "Nazis and Fascists and Japs." We would think that after Salinger had come under fire from the Germans, these life-threatening experiences would have reinforced his "Kill the Nazis" attitude. But they didn't.

7

Salinger's Job as a CIC Agent

In his biography *J. D. Salinger: A Life*, Kenneth Slawenski claims that Salinger regularly fought the Wehrmacht alongside the combat soldiers of the Twelfth Infantry Regiment: "Although an intelligence agent, once upon the field of battle, he was forced to become a leader of men, responsible for the safety and actions of squadrons [*sic*] and platoons. The lives of his fellow soldiers depended on the orders he gave."[1] This statement contains two errors of fact. First of all, Salinger's CIC detachment never participated in combat because they did rear echelon work well behind the front lines. Secondly, Salinger was not "a leader of men" responsible for squads and platoons. During the first three months after D-Day, he was a lowly corporal, and he did not regain his earlier rank as a staff sergeant until late in August 1944. Even as a staff sergeant in the CIC, he was not "a leader of men." The only soldier Salinger was responsible for was his driver, Corporal John Keenan.

What work Salinger's CIC detachment actually did can be learned from the After Action Reports of the Twelfth Regiment and the Periodic Reports (i.e., daily reports) of Salinger's CIC detachment. These records are kept at the National Archives in College Park, Maryland. The National Archives are also a treasure trove of various CIC publications, among them the thirty-volume *History of the Counter Intelligence Corps*. In this chapter I quote from those sources to show in detail what the role of Salinger's CIC detachment was within the Fourth Infantry Division and what kind of work the detachment actually did in France and Germany.

Salinger was assigned to the Twelfth Infantry Regiment of the Fourth Infantry Division, but his name does not appear on the personnel roster of that regiment.

Instead his name appears on the roster of the Fourth Division Headquarters Company, and so do the names of all the other agents of Salinger's CIC detachment.[2] This is because the CIC office was at the division headquarters, and the CIC agents were billeted with the headquarters company throughout the war. The division headquarters and command post, from which the commanding general issued his orders, was always located several miles behind the front lines and usually in a chateau, mansion, or some other substantial building.

Next, it is useful to know how Salinger's CIC detachment fit into the command structure of the Fourth Infantry Division. The division was commanded by Major General Raymond O. Barton (June to December 1944) and later by Brigadier General Harold W. Blakeley (December 1944 to October 1945). The division comprised the Eighth, the Twelfth, and the Twenty-Second Infantry Regiments. Each of those regiments numbered approximately 3,200 men and consisted of three battalions. Each battalion in turn comprised four rifle companies. In addition, the division included four field artillery battalions; an engineer, a medical, and a quartermaster battalion; plus the headquarters company and the CIC detachment.

According to volume 13 of *The History of the Counter Intelligence Corps*, on D-Day the Fourth Division CIC detachment consisted of two officers and fifteen enlisted men. The two officers were First Lieutenant Oliver Appleton and Second Lieutenant Bernard Boyce.[3] The enlisted men were a mix of sergeants, corporals, and PFCs (privates first class). The officers and a few of the enlisted men worked at division headquarters, but three groups of four enlisted men were assigned as field agents to the three regiments.

Corporal Salinger, corporals John Keenan and Jack Altaras, and PFC Paul Fitzgerald were the field agents nominally responsible for the Twelfth Infantry Regiment, but their work overlapped with that of the teams responsible for the Eighth and Twenty-Second Regiments. The field agents reported to the commanding officer of the detachment, Lieutenant (and later Captain) Appleton, whose office was at divisional headquarters. This meant that they regularly shuttled back and forth between divisional headquarters, usually over five miles from the front, and their regiments' command posts, usually within two miles of the fighting.

The History and Mission of the Counter Intelligence Corps in World War II explains what the duties of CIC detachments were. According to that 1946 Army publication, it was the task of the CIC "to combat espionage, sabotage, and subversion; to prevent leakage of information to the enemy; and to deliver security lectures to the troops." More specifically, the document states, "Counter Intelligence Corps detachments were to perform tactical Counter Intelligence Corps functions, such as search of enemy command posts and the questioning of civilians, informers, and agents in occupied territory. The Army detachment was to conduct *rear echelon* missions including safeguarding military information, security against the activities of enemy agents and *rear echelon* counter intelligence functions in general."[4] What kind of rear-echelon work Salinger's CIC detachment performed was reported by Salinger's commanding officer, Lieutenant Oliver Appleton, two days after D-Day:

> Agents of this Detachment accompanied by three Agents of the VII Corps, CIC Det., and a representative of the CAO [Civilian Affairs Office], 4th Inf. Div., went to St. Mere-Eglise [*sic*] for the purpose of setting up adequate security measures regarding civilians of that town. Upon arrival, the Mayor of the town informed us that representatives of CAO, 82nd Air-Borne Division and CIC Agents of the same Division had already set up security measures in the town. It was determined that telephone lines had been severed. Letters at the Post Office were impounded and turned over to CIC Det., VII Corps. Necessary proclamations were posted at the Town Hall. The Mayor of the town assured these Agents that he would encourage the civilian population to return to their homes and that the local police consisting of five policemen would establish the necessary road security measures in that town to prevent the free movement of civilians. VII Corps CIC Det. relieved CIC Det. 4th Inf. Div. from further duties in connection with the town of St. Mere-Eglise.[5]

In addition, Lieutenant Appleton reported that enemy installations were visited at the small towns of St. Martin and Beuzeville au Plain and that "Agents from this Detachment visited various MP Control Posts in order to check the instructions MPs were giving civilians." These instructions were that "the policy of the Division is for civilians to remain at home until the urgency of the military situation has passed."[6]

In connection with Salinger's CIC detachment checking on the work of the military police, I want to point out the special status of the CIC in the US Army. CIC agents did not wear rank insignia because they always had to deal with noncoms and officers who outranked them. If MP sergeants or lieutenants knew that Salinger was only a corporal, they might resent him for reminding them to obey security regulations and to safeguard military information. In the frontispiece of this book, Salinger is still wearing the staff sergeant's rank insignia on his sleeves that he wore before he joined the CIC.

In addition to not wearing rank insignia, another difference between CIC agents and other soldiers was that they were only lightly armed. All Salinger and his fellow CIC field agents had for protection were .45 caliber handguns. Why CIC agents needed to be armed at all becomes clear from the following

CIC agents searching for Nazi documents. Note that the men do not wear rank insignia on their tunics. (James Gilbert et al., *Under the Shadow of the Sphinx*)

Colt .45 handgun like Salinger's (Sam Lisker photo)

warning that Lieutenant Appleton issued in his June 13, 1944, report: "Considerable number of German soldiers are changing into civilian cloths [*sic*]. These soldiers are posing as French civilians and plan to allow American soldiers to pass by them and then either throw a hand grenade at them or shoot them in the back."[7]

No agents of Salinger's CIC detachment ever got into situations where they had to defend themselves against German soldiers or spies. But there were several occasions when they captured enemy soldiers who had been overlooked by the advancing combat troops. For instance, on June 11, 1944, Salinger's CIC unit captured four wounded German soldiers left behind in a fortified position half a mile east of Azeville, and on June 23, 1944, "one German prisoner was captured in a pill box about three miles to the southwest of Valognes."

The most important fact I discovered about Salinger's work as a CIC agent is that no one in his CIC detachment ever participated in combat. If they had, this would have been mentioned in the daily reports of Salinger's CIC detachment and in the After Action Reports of the Twelfth Infantry Regiment.

But Salinger was apparently ashamed at having been a rear-echelon soldier because he made statements to give the impression that he had spent a lot of time near the front and that his life was in constant jeopardy. In an August 1944 letter to an old college friend, Terry Glassmoyer (née Thierolf), Salinger wrote that he was "scared stiff constantly," and he said, "I dig my fox-holes to a cowardly depth."[8] And in a November 1944 contributor's note that appeared when *Story* magazine published "Once a Week Won't Kill You," Salinger says, "Am still writing whenever I can find the time and an unoccupied foxhole."[9] In both of these statements, Salinger suggests that he was hunkered down in foxholes almost as often as the combat soldiers were.

For those who have not served in the military, it might be useful to understand exactly what a foxhole is. Officially called a "Defensive Fighting Position," a foxhole is a narrow hole in the ground about six feet deep that allows a soldier not only to take cover from enemy fire but also to fight back from it. A good foxhole is wider at the bottom than at the top so that the soldier can curl up and sleep in it when he needs to.

Given the nature of his noncombat duties as a CIC agent, Salinger probably never dug his own foxhole. But during his visits to the command post of his Twelfth Regiment, it would have occurred occasionally that the regiment came under German artillery or mortar fire as it does in the story "The Stranger." On such occasions, Salinger and his driver, Keenan, would have ducked into foxholes until the shelling was over.

Even though the story "A Boy in France" shows Babe Gladwaller spending the night in a foxhole, I don't think Salinger ever had to. He and his CIC detachment shared the safe accommodations of the Fourth Division's headquarters company, which were always located miles behind the front.

There is an incident that supports my belief that Salinger never spent a night in a foxhole. This incident occurred during the Battle of the Hürtgen Forest. Salinger had an argument with Captain Appleton, the commanding officer of his CIC detachment. Appleton got so angry that he ordered Salinger to spend the night in one of the foxholes of the Twelfth Infantry Regiment. If Salinger had frequently spent nights in foxholes, then Appleton's order would not have been much of a punishment.

Here is how this story is reported by Werner Kleeman, one of the Fourth Division's German interpreters: "It was about 9PM and Salinger was told to go and stay in the foxhole with his regiment for the night. I felt sorry for him, and then remembered the blanket I had pinched from the Hotel Atlantique. I gave it to him, along with a pair of woolen socks that my mother had knitted and sent to me. He thanked me and left. The next day when I met up with him, I asked, 'How was the night?' He told me that, contrary to the captain's orders, he had found a place to sleep in a house a few blocks away and did not, in fact, go to the regiment to sleep in the soggy, snow-filed foxhole!"[10]

To appreciate this story, it is important to know that the house where Salinger spent the night was in Zweifall, the village where the Fourth Division headquarters company and the CIC detachment were housed. The nearest foxholes of the Twelfth Regiment were—according to the regiment's combat history—approximately three miles southeast of Zweifall.

Some of Salinger's duties as a CIC agent were no more interesting than impounding letters at the post offices, checking identification papers of suspicious civilians, and doing jeep patrols to keep civilians away from military installations and from the front. More interesting were his postbattle duties of retrieving documents from destroyed enemy command posts and dead enemy soldiers. But according to the daily reports of his CIC detachment, Salinger and the other field agents of his detachment occasionally also arrested German spies, members of the SS, and Nazi Party officials. Two experiences like these are reflected in "A Girl I Knew" and in "For Esmé—With Love and Squalor." In "A Girl I Knew" one of Salinger's alter egos interrogates a soldier who claims to be a sergeant in the regular German army but turns out to be a member of the SS. And in "For Esmé," Sergeant X arrests a woman who was a minor official in the Nazi Party. I will discuss these stories in later chapters.

8

The Saint-Lô SNAFU
and the Liberation of Paris

During the breakout of the invasion forces from the Cotentin Peninsula, Salinger witnessed another major debacle caused by the military leadership: the bombing of American troops by the Eighth US Air Force. Despite these self-inflicted casualties, the US Army was able to breach the German defenses and advance to Paris without encountering the fierce resistance the Wehrmacht had mustered at Cherbourg and Saint-Lô. The first American troops to enter Paris were the soldiers of Salinger's Fourth Infantry Division. Salinger was elated about being part of a second major historical event after the D-Day landings, but he also registered his first misgivings about the war. He expressed these doubts both in person to Ernest Hemingway and in a letter to his literary mentor Whit Burnett.

After the D-Day landings, it took the US Army twenty days to advance to the tip of the Cotentin Peninsula and annihilate the German garrison in the seaport of Cherbourg. They encountered equally stiff resistance when they tried to break out of the peninsula. It took them another twenty-two days to drive the Wehrmacht out of the city of Saint-Lô, fifty miles south of Cherbourg. That battle cost the US Army over five thousand casualties, and it resulted in the almost complete destruction of the city. As an anonymous GI remarked, "We sure liberated the hell out of this place."[1]

After occupying what was left of Saint-Lô, the US Army was unable to gain any ground on the Wehrmacht. To break the stalemate, General Omar Bradley, the commander of US forces in northern Europe, developed a radical plan code-named Operation Cobra. This operation involved a huge armada of bombing planes that were to breach the German lines. But that decision had fatal consequences.

According to Bradley's plan, 1,500 B-17 and B-24 heavy bombers, 380 medium bombers, and 350 fighter-bombers (both American and British) were to participate in the carpet-bombing of the German defenses. This operation turned into a fiasco because of two misunderstandings between General Bradley and the air force generals.

The US Army's official historian Martin Blumenson explains: "Bradley recommended that the planes make their bomb runs laterally across the front, parallel to the front lines, instead of approaching over the heads of American troops and perpendicular to the front." To prevent Americans being hit by stray bombs, Bradley had planned to withdraw the troops eight hundred yards from the bombing line. But the air force generals "demurred at making lateral bomb runs and objected to the slender 800-yard safety factor." They argued that approaching the target area laterally "would cause congestion over the target and make the completion of the attack impossible in the brief time required." And although the front ran along the Saint-Lô–Périer highway, which offered the pilots an excellent landmark, "the air chiefs wished a true safety ground factor of 3,000 yards."[2] There was some bargaining between Bradley and the air force generals that ended with each side thinking they had made a convincing argument. The upshot was that the air force made the bomb runs perpendicular to the front line and tried to use a 1,500-yard safety factor. But none of that mattered because Operation Cobra became a major military SNAFU (Situation Normal—All Fucked Up).

The bombings were scheduled to take place on July 24. But the weather was so unstable that they were postponed, except that the officer in charge of air operations, British air marshal Leigh-Mallory, called off the bombings too late. Most of the huge fleet of planes had already taken off from England, including the 1,500 heavy bombers, and they did not get word that the mission had been canceled because they had been given the wrong radio frequencies. Due to poor visibility, many of the planes turned around anyway, but some of them accidentally dropped their bombs on American positions rather than on the German lines. This resulted in 156 American casualties: 131 wounded and twenty-five killed.[3]

Undeterred by the reports of American casualties during the first abortive attack, General Bradley did not change the orders for the air force for the following day. The weather was clearer but there were even more American casualties this time. As the official record shows: "Fragmentation bombs and high explosives from 35 heavy bombers and the bombs of 42 medium bombers dropped within American lines." The casualties included 490 wounded and 111 killed. In addition, "Many individuals who suffered no visible physical injuries sustained concussions and shock. The 30th Division, for example, reported 164 cases of combat exhaustion attributable to the short bombing on 25 July."[4]

The regiment that sustained the most casualties was the Eighth Infantry Regiment, the unit that Salinger went ashore with on D-Day. An unusual fatality was visiting general Lesley McNair, who had come from Eisenhower's head-quarters to observe the bombings. He was the highest-ranking American officer to be killed in World War II.

In his book *The Americans at Normandy*, the military historian John McManus expresses the opinion that General Bradley was responsible for the unnecessary casualties of Operation Cobra. McManus says about Bradley: "He could have agreed to withdraw his troops farther back from the bombing line (another 1,000 yards would have made the difference). He could have, and should have, made sure his ground troops were well dug in, well spread out, and prepared for the possibility of short bombs." And McManus concludes: "Bradley failed to understand the limitations and perils of strategic bombers in support of ground troops."[5]

James Carafano comes to an even more damning conclusion. In his book *After D-Day: Operation Cobra and the Normandy Breakout*, Carafano writes: "A thorough review of the evidence suggests not only that General Bradley must bear major responsibility for the disaster, but that his failure was more than simply inexperience or an inadvertent lack of oversight." Carafano is sure that Bradley "knew the front line troops would take casualties. He was willing to take that risk."[6]

During the bombings near Saint-Lô, Salinger's Twelfth Regiment was camped in a concealed bivouac near the village of Le Perrey, ten miles northwest of Saint-Lô and five miles north of the highway that was the bombing line.[7] That location is from where Salinger probably watched the earth-shaking spectacle of over two thousand American and British planes dropping their bombs. After the ambulances came in with the wounded, Salinger must have spoken with the survivors of the Eighth Regiment. It is also likely that his CIC detachment was again ordered—as they were after the Slapton Sands disasters—to keep the information about the debacle from spreading because it would have lowered the morale of the entire army.

After the breakout from the Cotentin Peninsula on July 25, the US Army encountered only weak resistance during their advance to Paris, 189 miles to the south of Saint-Lô. The first American troops entered Paris on August 25, 1944. They were soldiers of Salinger's Fourth Infantry Division.

While Salinger was in Paris, three important things happened in his life: He met Hemingway, he was unable to save the life of a suspected Nazi collaborator he had arrested, and he made his first negative comments about the war and the army. Salinger described his meeting with Hemingway in a letter to his mentor Burnett, he mentioned the lynching of the suspected Nazi collaborator only to his daughter, Margaret, and he revealed his misgivings about the war both in his letter to Burnett and in a conversation with Hemingway.

Salinger's letter of September 9, 1944, written two weeks after the liberation of Paris, is the only joyful letter he wrote from Europe during or after World War II. He writes to Burnett that there was still shooting in the streets when he got to Paris, but "it was really fine": "The Parisian people make things seem more worthwhile. They cried, they laughed, they kissed us, they brought glasses of cognac up to the jeep, held their babies up for us for kissing. . . . If we had stood on top of the jeep and taken a leak, Paris would have said, 'Ah, the darling Americans. What a charming custom.'"[8]

When we compare Salinger's description of the delirious happiness of the Parisians to a similar account by the famous war correspondent Ernie Pyle, we will see that Salinger was not exaggerating. Like Salinger, Pyle rode through the crowded streets of Paris in a jeep, and he reported: "Once the jeep was simply swamped in human traffic and had to stop; instantly we were swarmed over and hugged and kissed and torn at. Everybody, even beautiful girls, insisted on kissing you on both cheeks. Somehow, I got started kissing babies that were held up by their parents."[9]

Salinger's description of the ecstatic reception of the American troops by the people of Paris is only slightly more giddy than that of his visit with Hemingway. Hemingway was staying at the exclusive Ritz Hotel and acted like royalty receiving the adulation of the commoners. Nevertheless Salinger wrote that he liked him very much: "He's very soft; not at all big-shotty or patronizing, and he's modest without affectation." More important, Salinger found that Hemingway "likes all the writers I do and disapproves of the ones I do."[10] Above all, Salinger reported that Hemingway had told him that he liked his story "Last Day of the Last Furlough," which had just come out in the *Saturday Evening Post*. Hemingway was not merely flattering Salinger: in the 1961 *Time* magazine feature article "Sonny—An Introduction," John Skow reported that Hemingway later said about Salinger, "Jesus, he has a helluva talent."[11]

Liberation: French woman dancing with a GI

In the letter about his time in Paris, Salinger did not mention the Nazis, except indirectly when he said that there was still some shooting in the streets. But in a conversation with his daughter, Margaret, Salinger related an incident involving the lynching of a suspected Nazi collaborator. This incident seems to have troubled him for a long time. Margaret reports: "My father told me that when he and his Jeepmate John Keenan arrested a suspected collaborator, the crowd spotted the man, tore him from their arms, and beat him to death on the spot. My father said there was nothing, short of gunning down the entire crowd, that they could have done to stop them."[12] According to Margaret's account of the incident, Salinger's impulse was to stop the lynching. That impulse would be natural to most Americans because in the United States we believe that everyone should be considered innocent until proof of guilt is established by a court of law.

We also need to consider that in his work as a CIC agent, Salinger had encountered numerous cases of French citizens falsely denouncing others as Nazi collaborators. For instance, on June 22, 1944, the daily report of Salinger's CIC detachment states that two members of the French Resistance denounced the owner of a bar in Valognes, Marie-Sireese Muller, as a Nazi collaborator. They also claimed that she had in her possession a German rifle and five rounds of ammunition. But the interrogation of the woman revealed that "Mme. Muller is nothing but a common prostitute whose affiliation with the Germans was purely on a professional basis."[13] Following up on such denunciations made up a large part of Salinger's work in France. Many of those denunciations turned out to be motivated by spite or self-interest rather than facts.

The lynching of the suspected Nazi collaborator in Paris must have troubled Salinger for years until he finally told his daughter about it. For all he knew, the man might have been innocent.

Joyful though Salinger's Paris letter sounds, it contains a jarring note. I noticed it only after rereading the letter several times. Near the beginning of the letter, Salinger said that the Parisian people and their happiness at being liberated "make things seem more worthwhile." Among the "things" that didn't seem to be "worthwhile" to Salinger must have been the heavy casualties that the US Army suffered at Saint-Lô and the unnecessary casualties during the bombing of American ground troops by the US Air Force.

Salinger shared his misgivings about the war with Hemingway. In a letter that Hemingway wrote to literary critic Malcolm Cowley on September 3,

1945, he mentioned Salinger's negative feelings about the war. Hemingway wrote: "We had a kid named Jerry Slasinger—no Salinger—in one of the C.I.C. teams in the division." And then Hemingway mentioned that Salinger "wanted to be a writer and wrote well" and that he "hated the army and the war."[14] Salinger's early doubts about the war and the army anticipate the explicit negative comments he made after the war.

So Salinger's happiness about witnessing the liberation of Paris and about getting to know Hemingway was tempered by two things. One was his inability to save a suspected Nazi collaborator from being beaten to death. The other was his feeling that fighting the Germans might not be worthwhile because of the enormous loss of lives. But I suspect that Salinger was also disturbed by the unnecessary deaths of American soldiers caused by American generals like Bradley at Saint-Lô.

9

The Hürtgen Forest Fiasco

The Battle of the Hürtgen Forest turned out to be an even greater debacle than Exercise Tiger at Slapton Sands and the bombing of US troops by the US Air Force at Saint-Lô. But this disaster did not affect Salinger as much because his CIC detachment did its work farther behind the front lines than usual and because the events unfolded over a period of three months, from September 19 to December 16, 1944. Salinger did not mention the battle in a letter he wrote to his friend Elizabeth Murray on November 28, 1944, even though he may have had a close call with death in the Hürtgen Forest. But he did turn that close call into fiction in the uncollected story "The Stranger."

Salinger did not mention the Battle of the Hürtgen Forest in his letter at all, not even by way of hints. This may be due in large part be to army censorship, but probably also to his excitement about his several meetings with Ernest Hemingway and his recent successes in placing his stories in American magazines. A war correspondent for the Fourth Infantry Division, Hemingway was housed in the same village where Salinger's CIC detachment was billeted.

The Battle of the Hürtgen Forest went down in history as the longest and costliest the US Army fought in World War II. The three-month battle cost the US Army thirty-three thousand casualties. The main reason for these catastrophic losses was that the American generals did not understand the enormous advantage the rugged terrain gave to the Germans.

The Hürtgen Forest, located just east of the border between Germany and Belgium, consists of fifty square miles of wooded ravines that are almost impossible for tanks, personnel carriers, and trucks to get through. Between September and December of 1944, the ground was either soaked by downpours or covered by snow, and visibility was often zero because of dense fog. These conditions canceled American superiority in air power, artillery, and tanks. And despite the fact that the American infantry outnumbered the Wehrmacht five to one, the terrain and the weather favored the Germans. Also, to stop the US Army before it even got to the Hürtgen Forest, the Germans had fortified the border between Germany and Belgium with a line of bunkers, tank traps, and mine-fields called the Siegfried Line.

The US Army, spearheaded by the Ninth Infantry Division, breached the Siegfried Line in September 1944. But then the American advance got bogged down due to the stiff resistance in the Hürtgen Forest. Before Salinger's Fourth Infantry Division joined the fighting in November, the German defenders had ground up two American infantry divisions, the Ninth and the Twenty-Eighth, and had denied the US Army any gains in territory. After the Fourth Infantry Division took over, it also suffered an appalling number of casualties before the Eighth Infantry Division relieved Salinger's Fourth and finally drove the Germans out of the Hürtgen Forest around Christmas.

In the larger scheme of things, the Battle of the Hürtgen Forest was a pyrrhic victory because while the US Army was tied down in the Hürtgen Forest, the Germans were able to assemble the thirty divisions that launched the Ardennes Offensive, later known as the Battle of the Bulge. The Ardennes Offensive was the only successful German operation after the D-Day invasion. The Wehrmacht pushed the US Army back sixty miles and inflicted even more casualties than they had at Hürtgen. Some twenty thousand GIs wound up in German prisoner of war camps, among them novelist Kurt Vonnegut.

Most military historians agree that the US Army should have bypassed the Hürtgen Forest and fought the Germans on terrain that was less of a disad-vantage to them. For instance, in the conclusion of the book *The Battle of the Huertgen Forest*, US Army historian Charles MacDonald writes, "Those in the Huertgen Forest fought a misconceived and basically fruitless battle that could have, and should have, been avoided."[1] The supreme commander of the Amer-ican forces in northern Europe, General Omar Bradley, even admitted in his autobiography *A General's Life* that the three-month battle did not achieve its objectives. He concluded, "To put it candidly, my plan to smash through to the Rhine and encircle the Ruhr [industrial area] had failed."[2]

In the smaller scheme of things, the Battle of the Hürtgen Forest was a disaster for Salinger's Twelfth Infantry Regiment. The regiment suffered a crippling number of casualties while being driven back by the Wehrmacht. The heavy casualties the Twelfth Regiment sustained were due to the decisions of a general who was unfamiliar with the difficult terrain and would not listen to the advice of the field officers.

This is how this disaster developed: General Leonard T. Gerow, commander of the Fifth Army Corps, decided to replace the badly mauled infantry regiment of another division with Salinger's Twelfth Infantry Regiment. Gerow issued a field order that called for the three battalions of the Twelfth Regiment to make separate attacks on three positions held by the Germans. As Colonel Gerden Johnson's *History of the Twelfth Infantry Regiment in World War II* records, the commander of Salinger's regiment, Colonel James S. Luckett, disagreed with that strategy: "Col. Luckett protested strongly against being required to make three divergent attacks, since the elements of the Twelfth Infantry would be out of contact with each other in addition to having no support on either flank."[3] Colonel Luckett pointed out that the rugged and densely forested terrain might allow the Germans to surround each battalion, something they would not be able to do if the battalions remained in physical contact. General Gerow overruled that objection. But something close to what Colonel Luckett had feared actually happened, and Hemingway comments on it his novel *Across the River and into the Trees.*

Hemingway begins his account of the fiasco with a briefing by General Walter Bedell Smith, whom Eisenhower's Supreme Headquarters Allied Expeditionary Force (SHAEF) had sent to raise the morale of the battered Twenty-Eighth Division and the reinforcements from the Fourth Division. Hemingway writes: "So after I had the privilege of hearing General Walter Bedell Smith explain the facility of the attack, we made it. . . . So we attacked, the three of us [the three battalions of the Twelfth Regiment] . . . exactly where the Germans wanted us to attack. We will not mention General Walter Bedell Smith any further. He is not the villain. He only made the promises and explained how it would go. . . . Nor the characters from SHAEF we never saw ever in these woods. Incidentally, and of course occurrences are always incidental at the SHAEF level, the [Twelfth] regiment was destroyed."[4]

The near destruction of the Twelfth Regiment occurred between November 10 and 12, when four companies of the regiment were encircled by Wehrmacht units. Each of those companies comprised approximately 150 men before the battle. When they retreated, there were only between twenty-five and fifty-five survivors in each company.[5] US Army historian MacDonald explains: "Not until November 15 . . . was Colonel Luckett able to extricate his four encircled companies and bring them back to a defensive line deep in the woods, almost the same line the 109th Infantry had used for its jump-off far back on the second day of November. In nine days of incredibly bitter fighting, the 12th Infantry had lost ground rather than gained it."[6]

The Twelfth Regiment began the Battle of the Hürtgen Forest with 3,142 officers and men and came out of the battle with 1,493 battle casualties (including more than seven hundred deaths) and 1,094 nonbattle casualties that were due chiefly to trench foot and frozen limbs. The *History of the Twelfth Infantry Regiment* states that due to these losses the regiment was "virtually lost to the Fourth Division."[7] In fact, the regiment was taken out of the fighting until it could be brought back up to combat strength by replacements.

To add insult to injury, General Gerow blamed Colonel Luckett for the disaster and relieved him of his command. Hemingway demonstrated his solidarity with Luckett when he wrote about him, "He was a man I would be glad to spend half my time in hell with."[8]

Throughout the Battle of the Hürtgen Forest, the Fourth Infantry Division's headquarters and the CIC detachment's offices were in a two-story stone building in the village of Zweifall. That village is located on the western edge of the Hürtgen Forest about five miles from where the heavy fighting occurred.

The daily CIC reports tell of the field agents' visits to American artillery positions and to villages a mile or more behind the front lines. Their tasks were to establish security for the American positions, to set up roadblocks in order to keep civilians away from the fighting, and to screen the local population for Nazi officials and for members of the Nazi Party. And fairly regularly, the CIC also interrogated German prisoners of war and passed tactical information to the intelligence and reconnaissance section of the Fourth Division.

In the letter from the Hürtgen Forest that Salinger wrote to Elizabeth Murray on November 28, 1944, he made no references directly or indirectly to the ferocity of the battle in which over half of his Twelfth Regiment were killed or wounded or had to be evacuated due to frozen hands or feet. Instead, he writes about his publishing triumphs and his visits with Hemingway.

For instance, Salinger mentioned that the *Saturday Evening Post* had accepted "A Boy in France" as well as three other stories and that *Story* magazine was going to publish "Elaine" and "Once a Week Won't Kill You." The rest of the letter deals mostly with Hemingway. Salinger said that he saw "the Farewell to Arms man quite often."[9] This was no exaggeration because Hemingway was staying in a private home in the village of Zweifall, just across the street from the CIC office. Werner Kleeman, an interpreter for the Fourth Division, went along on one of Salinger's visits. Kleeman reports that the three of them "sipped champagne from aluminum cups" and that neither he nor Salinger ever forgot Hemingway's kindness.[10]

In his letter to Murray, Salinger did indeed say that Hemingway was an

Former Fourth Infantry Division headquarters building in Zweifall (E. Alsen photo)

"exceptionally kind guy." But Salinger was "thumbs down on his philosophy or what have you." In particular, Salinger "hates" Hemingway's "overestimation of sheer physical courage commonly called guts," and he resented Hemingway's notion that F. Scott Fitzgerald was "a physical coward."

Much as I searched between the lines of this letter for clues that Salinger was disturbed about the horrific losses that his Twelfth Regiment sustained in the Battle of the Hürtgen Forest, I could find no such clues. This is odd because the story "The Stranger" suggests that Salinger himself came close to being killed at Hürtgen.

In "The Stranger," Babe Gladwaller, a Twelfth Regiment survivor, has returned to the United States after the end of the war and seeks out Helen, the former fiancée of his good friend Vincent Caulfield. He goes to see her because he wants to tell her how Vincent died.

After his return to the United States Gladwaller became obsessed by the idea that civilians don't really understand what the war was like because it is being misrepresented in movies and books. Salinger had already developed this idea in the earlier stories "Soft-Boiled Sergeant" and "Last Day of the Last Furlough." Gladwaller tells himself: "Don't let Vincent's girl think that Vincent asked for a cigarette before he died. Don't let her think he grinned gamely, or said a few choice last words. These things didn't happen. These things weren't done outside of movies and books."[11]

So Gladwaller tells Helen the truth about how Vincent died. It happened like this: Vincent, Gladwaller, and four other soldiers were standing around a fire in the perimeter of the Twelfth Regiment's command post in the Hürtgen Forest. Suddenly an enemy mortar shell exploded next to the group, and Vincent and three other soldiers were hit by shrapnel. Gladwaller says about Vincent: "He died in the medics' CP [command post] tent about thirty yards away, not more than about three minutes after he was hit." Then Gladwaller describes Vincent's death:

> I think he had too much pain in too large an area of his body to have realized anything but blackness. I don't think it hurt. I swear I don't. His eyes were open. I think he recognized me and heard me when I spoke to him, but he didn't say anything at all. The last thing he said was about one of us was going to have to get some wood for the lousy fire, preferably one of the younger men, he said, you know how he talked.[12]

The story reads like a lament for the death of someone Salinger may have known, and it makes a comment on the way the war affected the minds of soldiers. Vincent's death has deeply troubled Gladwaller. He apologizes twice to Helen, saying: "I don't know what's wrong with me since I'm back," and "I'm acting very peculiarly, I don't know what's the matter." What's wrong with Gladwaller is that—like Salinger—he is haunted by the many deaths he has witnessed in the war. All these deaths prey on his mind, as we can see in a passage where he remembers the four bloodiest battles he fought in and the many fellow soldiers who died in them. While Gladwaller is thinking of the trumpet playing of one of his favorite prewar jazz musicians, his mind suddenly jumps to "the music of the unrecoverable years; the little unhistorical, pretty good years when all the dead boys in the Twelfth Regiment had been living and cutting in on other dead boys on lost dance floors; the years when no one who could dance worth a damn had ever heard of Cherbourg or Saint Lô or Hürtgen Forest or Luxembourg." These seem to be Salinger's own thoughts, not those of Gladwaller. Although Salinger was not a combat soldier like Gladwaller, he also suffered psychic wounds when he had to do his work surrounded by the carnage after the battles of Cherbourg, Saint-Lô, Hürtgen Forest, and Luxembourg. Also like Gladwaller, Salinger may have had a close call in the Hürtgen Forest; the story of Vincent Caulfield being killed by mortar fragments may be based on something that happened during one of Salinger's regular visits to the Twelfth Regiment's command post.

General Barton visits the Twelfth Regiment command post in the Hürtgen Forest (Fourth Infantry Division Pictorial Record)

When I was exploring the Hürtgen Forest with camera operator Anthony Savini to shoot footage for Shane Salerno's movie *Salinger* (2013), I had the eerie experience of finding the tail section of a German mortar shell in an area where there had been a command post of Salinger's Twelfth Infantry Regiment. Unfortunately, none of that footage appears in the Salerno movie.

With the help of a Fourth Infantry Division map that I had copied at the National Archives, I found the location of one of the command posts. The trenches and foxholes were almost obliterated because their sides had caved in, but we could still tell that a particularly large, square depression in the ground must have been the dugout for the command post of regimental commander Colonel Luckett and his staff.

Not far from the center of the compound, I saw a metal object sticking out of the ground and picked it up. It was part of a mortar shell with the stabilizer fins. Because the battle in the Hürtgen Forest went back and forth, with the Germans often driving the Americans out of their positions only to be driven back the following day, the fragment I found could have been from either a German or an American mortar shell. Back at the hotel that evening, I went on the internet and brought up pictures of American and German 81mm mortar shells. Because the tail sections are very different, I identified the fragment I found as definitely being from a shell that the Wehrmacht had fired at the command post of Salinger's Twelfth Infantry Regiment. The thought occurred to me that this might have been the shell that killed Vincent Caulfield—or rather the unlucky GI whose death Salinger fictionalized in "The Stranger."

Perhaps Salinger did not narrowly escape death in the Hürtgen Forest. But his description of Gladwaller's unbalanced mental state reflects his own psychological stress. As Salinger reveals in a postwar letter that I will discuss later, he was as deeply troubled by the deaths of so many of his fellow soldiers as was Gladwaller. Gladwaller seems to have coped with all the deaths he witnessed by denial—that is, by deliberately ignoring the Germans who caused those deaths. He gives that impression because he doesn't ever mention any Nazis, Krauts, or Germans—not even in his inner monologues—even though the Germans killed his best friend, Vincent. Similarly, in his letter from the Hürtgen Forest, Salinger doesn't ever mention the Germans or the Nazis; nor does he even hint at the horrendous casualties the Wehrmacht was inflicting on his Twelfth Infantry Regiment. But Salinger's strategy of denial eventually failed him, and he suffered a nervous breakdown.

10

Searching for Nazi Spies and Collaborators in Luxembourg

The Battle for Luxembourg cost Salinger's Twelfth Infantry Regiment almost as many casualties as the Battle of the Hürtgen Forest. The regiment was especially hard hit during the action around the town of Echternach. That town is located on the Sauer River, twenty-one miles northeast of Luxembourg City. During the Echternach battle—which raged from December 16 to 24, 1944—the Twelfth Regiment lost a whole company that was taken prisoner by the Germans. But the regiment held the town and prevented the Wehrmacht from advancing toward the city of Luxembourg. The Battle for Echternach was part of Field Marshal Gerd von Rundstedt's preparation for the Ardennes Offensive, also known as the Battle of the Bulge.

During the Battle for Echternach, Salinger's family and friends did not hear from him for over a week and were worried that he might have been killed or captured. But they need not have worried because Salinger was nowhere near the fighting. Salinger refers to this battle in the story "Blue Melody" (1948).

When I first read about the Battle for Echternach, I ran across some information that suggested Salinger's CIC detachment might actually have fought there. In the *History of the Twelfth Infantry Regiment in World War II*, Colonel Gerden Johnson reports that after his regiment suffered massive casualties, they were desperately short-staffed and had to retreat: "Sixty cooks, orderlies, and military police from Division Headquarters were attached to a battalion of the 12th to reinforce the new line [of defense]."[1]

Since Salinger's CIC detachment was part of the divisional headquarters company, I thought, "Aha, this is were Salinger finally got a chance to shoot back at the Germans." But when I studied the daily reports of his CIC detachment and the After Action Reports of the Twelfth Infantry Regiment, I found that between December 8 and 27 Salinger's CIC detachment was billeted in Luxembourg City, twenty-one miles southwest of Echternach, and that the command post of Salinger's Twelfth Infantry Regiment was in the village of Junglinster, eleven miles from where the fighting was going on.

The daily reports of Salinger's CIC detachment show that during the battle of Echternach the agents were working mostly in Luxembourg City and the surrounding small towns and villages. On December 7, 1944, Salinger's boss, Captain Oliver Appleton, reported that "Agents of this detachment took over the duties of the 83rd CIC Detachment in the City of Luxembourg" and that "offices were established at Mondorf, Senningen, and Junglinster."[2] These are villages on the northeastern and southeastern periphery of Luxembourg City. Appleton also mentioned that "motor patrols were made within the division area for the purpose of checking all civilians and suspicious appearing soldiers encountered."[3] These motor patrols came closest to the front when they operated in the villages of Consdorf and Zittig, both about six miles west of Echternach.

The CIC motor patrols were not unimportant busy work, because during the Battle of the Bulge German Counter Intelligence, the Abwehr, made a concerted effort to disrupt American defenses. This is explained in a book published by the Army Intelligence and Security Command titled *In the Shadow of the Sphinx: A History of Army Counterintelligence*: "Dressed in US uniforms and equipped with captured weapons and jeeps, enemy soldiers of the Einheit Stielau were to perform intelligence collection, commit acts of sabotage, and sow confusion. To give the plan a chance of success, German leaders selected English-speaking soldiers for participation and provided them an intense orientation to American culture to include watching of newsreels and movies, learning current slang words, and practicing American mannerisms, such as the handling of cigarettes."[4]

The CIC caught on quickly after they arrested three German soldiers posing as Americans: "Failing to give the correct password, three members of a [Stielau] team were apprehended wearing US uniforms and possessing a jeep and sabotage devices." Thereafter, the CIC intensified its motor patrols and set up additional roadblocks. This seems to have worked because the commander of the Einheit Stielau, Lieutenant Colonel Otto Skorzeny, admitted during the Dachau war crimes trials that only two of his teams survived and only one of them brought back worthwhile information.[5] Twenty-three of his men were caught and executed by the CIC (one of them was the best friend of my uncle Dietrich Kukla). However, Salinger's CIC detachment did not intercept any Germans in American uniforms and was not involved in any executions.

As far as Salinger's CIC work in Luxembourg City is concerned, Captain Appleton reported that one of the more unusual jobs of the detachment was "a survey of all the waiters in the City of Luxembourg" and that "several of the waiters were interrogated and warned that the first report of any adverse information against them would mean their immediate arrest."[6] Another aspect of the work of Salinger's CIC detachment that was different in Luxembourg from what they had been used to was their cooperation with the Luxembourg Gendarmerie and Sûreté. As Captain Appleton reported: "Arrangements were made to have an agent at the Sûreté Office at all times" to double check all cases in which "permission to travel was granted to civilians."[7]

Although little of the work of Salinger's CIC detachment in Luxembourg was noteworthy, they did make one spectacular arrest when they apprehended a Nazi spy outside the command post of the Eighth Regiment. This happened on January 1, 1945, a week after the Battle for Echternach. The spy's name was Marcel Silberseisen, or perhaps Silbereisen, and his instructions were as follows: "Subject was . . . to find out especially how many armored units there were in the area, their unit numbers and strength in men and weapons, whether or not they were fully motorized, and their locations; also the location of any other units observed."[8]

This arrest made up for the CIC's failure to apprehend any Nazi spies before the Echternach battle. That earlier failure, so the *History of the Twelfth Infantry Regiment in World War II* states, had given a big advantage to the Wehrmacht: "The enemy apparently had considerable detailed information of our positions—probably obtained through local espionage. . . . It was obviously easy for German agents to circulate among the largely German-speaking population of Luxembourg, and in spite of all efforts of the counter-intelligence corps, it is believed that there were a large number of such agents."[9]

The reason Salinger's CIC detachment did not arrest Nazi spies in the Echternach area was that the detachment did most of their work in Luxembourg City. After the Twelfth Regiment had repelled the attack on the town of Echternach, the Ardennes Offensive had passed Luxembourg by, giving the city up without a fight so that it was totally untouched by the war. While the Battle of the Bulge was going on for one more month some thirty miles to the north, it must have felt like peacetime in Luxembourg City. Having been previously billeted in cities that had been reduced to rubble, Salinger's CIC detachment must have found Luxembourg City to be a paradise.

There seems to have been quite a bit of partying in Luxembourg City during the Battle of the Bulge. For instance, Leicester Hemingway mentions that he

Cafés around the Place d'Armes, Luxembourg City

met J. D. Salinger at a party at a posh Luxembourg hotel. In his book *My Brother Ernest Hemingway*, Leicester reports that during that party Ernest was relaxing with a group of people that included "Jerome Salinger, who was a good CIC man for the division."[10] Leicester apparently got to know Salinger quite well because after the war he visited him in the Bavarian town of Weißenburg, where Salinger's CIC detachment was posted with the Army of Occupation.

Salinger mentions the Battle of Luxembourg in the story "Blue Melody," published in the September 1948 issue of *Cosmopolitan*. That story is not about the war. It takes place in Tennessee and deals with the fictional African American blues singer Lida Louise. The gist of the story is that Lida's appendix burst and she died because she was denied treatment at an all-white hospital (this is a riff on the death of blues singer Bessie Smith). The war is mentioned only in the introduction of "Blue Melody," when the narrator tells us that he heard the story of Lida Louise from another soldier in Luxembourg.

The situation in the introduction of the story is similar to that in the unpublished "Magic Foxhole." As in "The Magic Foxhole," an anonymous soldier hitches a ride on an army vehicle that is on the way to the front. As in "The Magic Foxhole," this anonymous soldier will be getting off the vehicle before it gets to its destination. Also as in "The Magic Foxhole," there is a strong suggestion that the hitchhiker is an alter ego of Salinger. Here is how "Blue Melody" begins: "In mid-winter of 1944 I was given a lift in the back of an overcrowded GI truck, going from Luxembourg City to the front at Halzhoffen, Germany [this would be Echternach; no town named Halzhoffen exists]—a distance of four flat tires, three (reported) cases of frozen feet, and at least one case of incipient pneumonia."[11]

Notice that the narrator comes from Luxembourg City, where Salinger's CIC detachment was quartered, and that he hitches a ride, which means he is not part of the unit that's on the way to the front. And unlike the other occupants of the truck, he is not a combat soldier. That comes out when he says that "the forty-odd men jammed in the truck were nearly all infantry replacements" who had been wounded earlier in the war and were now being sent back into action. In short, this alter ego of the CIC agent Salinger is trying to get to his regimental command post at Junglinster, about halfway between Luxembourg City and the front.

The last paragraph of the introduction to "Blue Melody" confirms the supposition that the narrator is Salinger because he reveals a negative attitude toward the war and the army that is similar to what Salinger had expressed in conversations and letters. When talking about the story he is about to tell, the narrator says, "It's just a simple little story of Mom's apple pie, ice-cold beer, the Brooklyn Dodgers, and the Lux Theater of the Air—the things we fought for, in short."[12] In this statement Salinger suggests that the US Army did not fight the war to defeat the genocidal ideology of the Nazis and their imperialist ambitions. Instead the US Army fought the war to impose American values on Europe, and Salinger's narrator identifies those values as kitschy patriotism (Mom's apple pie), consumerism (ice-cold beer), baseball (the Brooklyn Dodgers), and the use of radio to advertise products such as soap (the Lux Theater of the Air).

It was in "Blue Melody," published in September 1948, that Salinger's subversive ideas about the war appeared in print for the first time. But he had expressed doubts about the war as early as August 1944 in a conversation with Ernest Hemingway and again in September 1944 in a letter to his mentor Whit Burnett. And he most emphatically expressed his unpatriotic ideas in a letter he wrote shortly after his nervous breakdown in May 1945, when he called the war "a tricky, dreary farce" and admitted that his thoughts about the US Army were "edgy with treason."

Salinger's negative feelings about the war and the army had been simmering ever since the Saint-Lô and Hürtgen Forest disasters. By the time he wrote "Blue Melody"—probably sometime in 1947 or 1948—these negative feelings had become so strong that Salinger blanked out the fact that the US Army had been fighting a country that had enslaved all of Europe and exterminated millions of human beings. How else to explain that in "Blue Melody" Salinger never mentions the Nazis, the Krauts, or the Germans but innocuously refers to them as "the enemy"?

11

Visit to a Concentration Camp

Ten days before the end of the war, J. D. Salinger became a Holocaust witness. In her book *Dream Catcher*, Salinger's daughter, Margaret, reports: "As a counter-intelligence officer, my father was one of the first soldiers to walk into a certain, just liberated, concentration camp. He told me the name, but I no longer remember." Margaret also quotes her father as saying, "You never really get the smell of burning flesh out of your nose entirely, no matter how long you live."[1] Salinger never mentioned this horrifying experience anywhere else, and his only reference to a concentration camp in his fiction is problematic.

After studying maps of the locations of all concentration camps in southern Germany and of the locations of all command posts of Salinger's Twelfth Infantry Regiment as it advanced into Bavaria, I concluded that the camp Salinger walked into was Kaufering Lager IV near Landsberg. This was one of eleven small satellite camps of the main camp at Dachau, located forty-five miles to the east.

I had no idea that there were over 1,600 such small camps in Germany. No one ever mentioned those small camps while I was growing up there. As Paul Fussell explains in his book *The Boys' Crusade: The American Infantry in Northwestern Europe, 1944–1945*, these small camps were slave labor camps and not "such industrialized killing institutions as Auschwitz-Birkenau." Fussell writes:

> The slave labor camps were in Germany proper, and their function was to
> provide workers, no matter how badly treated, for crucial industries [the
> prisoners at the Kaufering camps were forced to build two gigantic under-
> ground aircraft hangars]. The function of the other kind of camps was
> quite different. They were not in Germany but all in Poland, as if their
> operations were admittedly too nasty to be associated with high German

purpose. . . . In short, the function of the death camps was to forward the Final Solution of the Jewish problem . . . by subjecting to Zyklon B gas the men, women, and children from all over Europe who would [otherwise] increase the Jewish population.[2]

Kaufering Lager IV was labeled the *Krankenlager*, the camp for the sick of the other ten Kaufering camps. But it was really an extermination camp because the sick prisoners, most of them Jews from Eastern Europe, did not receive any medical attention. Instead they were left to die from their sicknesses or from starvation.

Soldiers of the US Army's Twelfth Armored Division discovered Kaufering Lager IV around noon on April 27, 1945. At that time some of the camp's buildings were still burning. On the previous day, April 26, the last eight hundred prisoners who were well enough to travel had been loaded onto railroad cattle cars to be transported to the main camp at Dachau. The morning of April 27, just before the SS guards abandoned the camp, they had a tank truck spray gasoline on the roofs of the eight earthen huts that housed the prisoners who were too sick to be evacuated. Then the SS set those huts on fire.[3]

Salinger was not one of the first American soldiers to enter the Kaufering camp as his daughter suggests. The German holocaust historian Anton Posset reports that after Colonel Edward Seiller of the Twelfth Armored Division got a radio message about the camp, he immediately went to see it, and he, together with "officers of the counter intelligence were the first [American] soldiers to come into the concentration camp Kaufering IV."[4] These CIC officers must have been from Seiller's Twelfth Armored Division because Salinger's Fourth Infantry Division was operating about twenty miles northwest of the camp at the time. Salinger probably went to see the camp on April 28, a day after its discovery.

Having examined the written reports of several American soldiers, dozens of photos, and Kaufering movie footage taken by the US Army Signal Corps, I can offer the following reconstruction of what Salinger must have smelled and seen when he walked into Kaufering Lager IV.

For quite some distance before he entered the camp, Salinger would have smelled the stench of burned bodies. Sergeant Robert T. Hartwig remembers that when he and another GI drove their jeep through the village of Hurlach, about a mile from the Kaufering camp, they knew they were "near a camp site because of the sickening odor of burning bodies," and Corporal Pete Bramble reports that "the stench was terrible, especially the burning corpses."[5]

When Salinger came to the gate of the camp, he would have seen a sign on the guardhouse proclaiming in German that nobody was allowed to enter because of *Seuchengefahr*, the danger of infection due to typhus. Entering the camp, Salinger would have walked past rows of dead prisoners on both sides of a central passageway. Here is Colonel Julien Saks's description:

> We entered and looked around. We were so shocked at what we saw that we couldn't say a word. I walked down one of the short streets and counted 65 bodies lying in ditches. The bodies were very emaciated, probably weighing no more than 50 to 75 pounds, and had been starved to death. . . . Many of the bodies had sores, as if the skin had contracted and cracked. The smell of death filled our nostrils. It was much worse than any pictures show, because the pictures don't show the odor or the sores on the bodies.[6]

Walking farther into the camp, Salinger would have come upon earthen huts on both sides. These huts were nothing but trenches dug into the ground and covered with roofs about forty feet long and twelve feet wide. The roofs had grass growing on them for camouflage. At one end of each earthen hut there was a window and at the other end was a door. Each hut held between fifty and sixty prisoners.

As Salinger approached the eight earthen huts that the SS had set on fire, the smell of burned flesh would have gotten stronger. Among the still-smoldering rafters, he would have seen and smelled the charred corpses of eighty-six prisoners. Next to the burned-down huts, he would have seen the bodies of prisoners who had crawled out of the burning hovels. As one eyewitness reports: "Many of the corpses were in a crawling posture with wounds both from guns and blunt weapons."[7]

If Salinger had walked through the large break in the barbed wire fence at the east end of the camp, he would have passed a small wooded area where he would have seen thirty-one more dead prisoners. The condition of those corpses was described by Major Charles P. Larson, who performed the autopsies. Larson reports that "examination of these bodies showed that 17 of them had died as a result of gunshot wounds; mostly multiple and probably from machine gun fire as whole extremities were amputated on some."[8]

Most of the dead prisoners in the wooded area east of the camp and near the railroad tracks had not been killed by the SS but were victims of a tragic mistake by the pilots of two American P-51 fighter-bombers. They saw a train parked on the tracks next to the Kaufering camp and assumed that it was a military train because it included a flatcar with two anti-aircraft guns mounted

Charred bodies at the Kaufering concentration camp (US Holocaust Museum)

on it. But the train had just been loaded with some eight hundred prisoners who were to be transported to the main camp at Dachau. The two planes raked the train with their machine guns in three strafing runs. The SS guards abandoned the train and sought shelter in the woods, and the prisoners who survived the attack escaped.

I found out about this tragedy from Anton Posset's article "The End of the Holocaust in Bavaria,"[9] and I learned additional details from two survivors of Kaufering Lager IV. One of them is Friedrich Schaffranek, with whom I conducted a telephone interview. The other survivor is Joseph Hausner, whose article titled "Strafing and Liberation" appears on the website of the Twelfth Armored Division. A filmed interview with Mr. Hausner can be seen on You-Tube.[10] The reports of Schaffranek and Hausner make it clear that it was the heavy machine gun fire from the two American airplanes that "amputated" whole extremities of some of the prisoners who died near the railroad tracks. Salinger, of course, could not have known about this tragedy. He must have assumed that those prisoners had also been killed by the SS guards.

Camp Commander Eichelsdörfer among scores of corpses (US Holocaust Museum)

The transcripts of the Dachau war crimes trials supply the most accurate Kaufering death count. According to those figures, Salinger would have seen the corpses of eighty-six prisoners who had been burned to death, plus 274 others of people had died from starvation or typhus or had been shot to death.[11]

    The number of dead prisoners Salinger saw at the small Kaufering camp is dwarfed by the thousands of bodies that American soldiers discovered at the

Buchenwald and Dachau camps. But despite the smaller number of bodies, Kaufering Lager IV was just as horrifying as Dachau and Buchenwald because of the stench of the burned corpses.

Footage of the camp can be seen on a seven-minute film that Colonel Seiller of the Twelfth Armored Division commissioned the US Signal Corps to make. It shows some 250 German civilians from the nearby city of Landsberg, whom Seiller ordered to bury the dead prisoners. This film can be seen on the website of the Landsberg citizens association that was formed to document the holocaust in Bavaria.[12]

We would expect that Salinger's horrifying experience at Kaufering IV might have left an explicit imprint in his stories. But his only reference to a concentration camp occurs in the story "A Girl I Knew," and this reference contains an error of historical fact.

In "A Girl I Knew," a CIC sergeant interviews civilians and prisoners of war in order to unmask disguised Nazi officials and members of the SS so they can be put on trial. In addition, Salinger's narrator has a personal agenda. Whenever he comes across Austrians, he asks them whether they know what happened to a Jewish girl from Vienna whom he knew before the war. Near the end of the story, the CIC sergeant meets a Jewish doctor who has just returned from the Buchenwald concentration camp, and that doctor tells him that the girl and her family "were burned to death in an incinerator."[13]

There is a problem with this incinerator remark. The Buchenwald camp was a labor camp and not an extermination camp like Auschwitz. It had five incinerators to cremate the thousands of prisoners who died due to malnutrition and unattended medical problems. Also some four thousand Russian prisoners of war who were murdered outright. But no one at Buchenwald was ever "burned to death in an incinerator." This was established beyond a doubt in *The Buchenwald Report*, commissioned by the US Army and written by former Buchenwald prisoner Albert G. Rosenberg.[14]

I suspect that it was actually not Salinger who wrote the statement about the Jewish family having been burned to death in an incinerator. "A Girl I Knew" was published in *Good Housekeeping*, and I would guess that it was the editors at *Good Housekeeping* who wrote the incinerator line because they also changed the title of the story without asking Salinger for permission. The original title of the story was "Wien, Wien" ("Vienna, Vienna"), which was also the title of a popular prewar song.[15] The change of the title was clearly an improvement because "Wien, Wien" was not something readers of *Good Housekeeping* could relate to. But the incinerator sentence amounts to a falsification of Holocaust history. This historical inaccuracy notwithstanding, "A Girl I Knew" occupies an important place in Salinger's work because it is his only story in which he mentions the Holocaust, even if only indirectly.

The astonishing thing about Salinger's visit to the Kaufering concentration camp is that it did not result in a change of his nonjudgmental attitude toward the Nazis or in a change of his negative attitude toward the war and the US Army. What he saw and smelled at the Kaufering camp did not make Salinger concede that the US Army had been fighting an evil of horrific proportions.

Instead, Salinger's visit to Kaufering Lager IV triggered a nervous breakdown. Apparently he was unable to push into a dark corner of his mind the sights and smells of so much death. Perhaps it also traumatized him that most of the dead prisoners were Jewish because he had all along tried to ignore the Holocaust.

12

Nervous Breakdown

Aweek after the end of the war, Salinger suffered a mental collapse. But it took him two months, until July 1945, to seek help in the psychiatric ward of a civilian hospital. He mentions his nervous breakdown in a letter he wrote to Ernest Hemingway from that hospital, and in "For Esmé—With Love and Squalor" he describes the symptoms of the nervous breakdown that the CIC agent Sergeant X suffers.

It is widely assumed that Salinger's nervous breakdown was a case of combat fatigue or shell shock. But Salinger was not a combat soldier. Also, he did not suffer his breakdown immediately after a life-threatening event but after the end of the war. Moreover Salinger uses the term *nervous breakdown* and not *combat fatigue* in his story about his alter ego Sergeant X.

Combat fatigue was fairly common among the soldiers of Salinger's Twelfth Infantry Regiment. For instance, in the combat history of the regiment, Colonel Gerden Johnson reports that after the Battle of Mortain in France "there were many cases of combat fatigue even among our older men."[1] And when war correspondent Ernie Pyle described the aftermath of the air force's accidental bombing of American troops at Saint-Lô, he mentioned that the Eighth Infantry Regiment—the outfit Salinger landed with in Normandy—had been hit especially hard by the bombing: "Their casualties, including casualties in shock, were heavy. Men went to pieces and had to be sent back."[2]

Salinger himself describes a case of "Battle Fatigue" (he spells it with capital letters) in his unpublished story "The Magic Foxhole." The story is about Lewis Gardner, a former lawyer, whose mind cracks during a two-day battle in which most of the men of his company were killed.

The main symptom of Gardner's nervous breakdown is a recurring hallucination. In a "magic foxhole," he claims to have met his as-yet-unborn son who is now twenty years old and is fighting in a war of the future. Two other symptoms of his nervous breakdown are that Gardner moves as though he is partially paralyzed and he looks as gray as a corpse. When he is evacuated to a field hospital on Utah Beach, he doesn't want to lie down on a stretcher but stands there like a statue holding on to a pole that the medics stuck in the sand for him.[3]

The cases of battle fatigue described by Colonel Johnson, Ernie Pyle, and Salinger have two things in common: the nervous breakdowns occurred immediately after the soldiers experienced life-threatening situations and these breakdowns made the men unable to fight. What was called battle fatigue or shell shock in World War II is now officially called acute stress disorder. It is an acute condition because it sets in immediately or very soon after a traumatic event.

A publication of the Committee on Gulf War and Health explains that if there is "a delayed onset of the symptoms" of acute stress disorder or "if the symptoms persist beyond a month, the person might meet the criteria for PTSD [posttraumatic stress disorder]." This publication further states that "most people who have PTSD also have other psychiatric disorders, such as major depressive disorders."[4] And the book that most psychiatrists regard as their bible, *The Diagnostic and Statistical Manual of Mental Disorders*, mentions that the traumas suffered by individuals with PTSD "include, but are not limited to, exposure to war as a combatant or civlian" and "witnessing atrocities."[5]

Salinger's nervous breakdown did not occur immediately after D-Day, nor after one of the other times he came under fire, nor immediately after his traumatic visit to the Kaufering concentration camp. This makes it a likely case of PTSD, especially since Salinger himself mentions "despondency" as one of its symptoms. And as I will explain later, even more severe effects of Salinger's PTSD were two related personality disorders.

In his letter to Hemingway, Salinger says that his nervous breakdown made him turn to "a General Hospital in Nuremberg." Because in 1945 no other hospital in Nuremberg had a psychiatric clinic, that hospital must have been the Klinikum Nord, then called the Allgemeines Städtisches Krankenhaus, the Municipal General Hospital. (By the way, this Nuremberg hospital happens to be where I was born six years before Salinger was treated there).

In July 1945, two months after the end of the war, Dr. Ulrich Fleck, a prominent Nazi, still remained director of the psychiatric clinic at this Nuremberg hospital. Dr. Fleck's file in the Nuremberg city archive shows that he had been a *Sturmbannarzt* (storm trooper doctor) of the paramilitary SA from 1933 to 1934 and a member of the Nazi Party from 1937 to 1945. In addition, he had been a member of several other Nazi organizations, including one that was affiliated with the SS.[6] And a who's who of important people in the Third Reich quotes the following statement from a letter Fleck wrote to a colleague in 1940: "It is true after all, with some patients who have been retarded since birth one thinks again and again it would almost be more humane to end their lives."[7] Here it seems that Fleck is advocating Hitler's euthanasia program, which ordered doctors to administer "mercy deaths" to the incurably sick.

Because Fleck must have been on the CIC's "Automatic Arrest" list, Salinger should have arrested him, but he didn't. The CIC finally took Fleck into custody on September 3, 1945, two months after Salinger had been a patient at his clinic. As soon as Fleck was gone, the clinic removed his portrait from the gallery of previous directors on the walls of the central staircase.

I visited the Nuremberg hospital with Anthony Savini, a camera operator for Shane Salerno's movie *Salinger*, and I interviewed the current head of psychiatry, Dr. Bernhard Jahn. Jahn told me that Haus 31, the building in which the psychiatric clinic is located, had changed very little since 1945, except that Fleck's portrait had been removed and so had the bars from most of the windows of the patients' rooms. Jahn could not confirm that Salinger had been a patient at his clinic because the hospital keeps its patients' records for only fifty years. He was pleased when I told him that I had proof that Salinger was treated there because in a letter to Hemingway he discussed his interaction with one of the clinic's psychiatrists.

In his letter to Hemingway, Salinger explained why he checked himself into that Nuremberg hospital. He said, "I've been in an almost constant state of despondency and I thought it would be good to talk to somebody sane." Salinger did not tell Hemingway what caused his nervous collapse, but he dropped some hints that point to the US Army as having caused his breakdown. When the German psychiatrist asked him if he liked the army, so Salinger told Hemingway, he answered, "I've always liked the Army." But later in the letter, Salinger reveals that he was kidding when he claimed he liked the Army. He said, "I'd give my right arm to get out of the Army, but not on a psychiatric, this-man-is-not-fit-for-Army-life ticket."[8] This comment explains why Salinger did not check himself into a US Army hospital. He did not want to risk the stigma of a psychiatric discharge from the army.

Salinger's deep disaffection for the army is revealed even more clearly in an earlier letter he wrote to his friend Elizabeth Murray.[9] This letter, written five

Size of .45 caliber bullets

days after the end of the war, reveals that the despondency he told Hemingway about was only a minor symptom of his nervous breakdown. Instead of appearing despondent in that letter, Salinger comes across as angry. Also there is a lunatic quality to the letter that makes me suspect Salinger wrote it right after his nervous collapse.

Near the beginning of the letter, Salinger refers to his "own little war over here" and says that it "will go on for some time." At first it's not clear what he meant by his "own little war." But then Salinger wrote, "My most casual thoughts over here are edgy with treason. It's a mess Elizabeth. Wonder if you have any idea." This suggests that his "own little war" was with the US Army.

The next paragraph of the letter explains why Salinger felt his thoughts were treasonous. He said that he was "delighted" that he had missed the VE-Day celebrations in the United States. He was especially happy that he had missed the ticker-tape parade in New York and "the sight of thousands of patriotic garment workers throwing raw woolens out of windows." And then Salinger explained what he did on the day Germany surrendered: "I celebrated the day wondering what close relatives would think if I fired a .45 slug neatly, but effectively through the palm of my left hand, and how long it would take me to learn to type with what was left of my hand."

At this point in the letter, we can have no idea why Salinger was not elated by the victory in Europe. His negative attitude toward the VE-Day celebrations seems not only unpatriotic but indeed "edgy with treason." Actually, the self-mutilation he contemplated would have been an act of treason because it would have landed him in a hospital and would have prevented him from doing his work as a CIC agent.

The next to last paragraph of the letter is even more subversive and more critical of the army than the previous ones. Salinger wrote: "I have three battle participation stars and am due a fourth, and I intend to have them all grafted onto my nostrils, two on each side. What a tricky, dreary farce, and how many men are dead." This passage shows that Salinger had no regard for the way the army rewards soldiers with medals. This is understandable because as a CIC agent he did not participate in any battles, and yet he was given four battle participation stars. But more important, Salinger ended that passage by calling World War II "a tricky, dreary farce." I take this to mean that Salinger did not believe that fighting Nazi Germany justified the deaths of so many men.

Now here is the paradox. Salinger's nervous breakdown was most likely triggered by his visit to the Kaufering concentration camp, the most recent traumatic event in his life. But the sights and smells of the burned corpses there did not convince Salinger that World War II was a "good war" or that the US Army had been fighting an evil of monstrous proportions.

The more I reread Salinger's crazy May 13, 1945, letter, the more I became convinced that his nervous breakdown was more damaging to his personality than the nervous breakdown of Sergeant X in "For Esmé—With Love and Squalor," and almost as serious as the nervous breakdown of ex-sergeant Seymour Glass, who commits suicide in "A Perfect Day for Bananafish."

"For Esmé—with Love and Squalor" is one of Salinger's two most autobiographical stories. It deals with the nervous breakdown of Sergeant X, a counter-intelligence sergeant at the end of World War II. In part one of the story, Sergeant X is being trained for the D-Day invasion at a British military intelligence school in the south of England. Part two takes place after the end of the war, when Sergeant X is part of the Army of Occupation and is stationed in Gaufurt, Bavaria, the fictional counterpart of the small town of Weißenburg, where Salinger was stationed.

Even though Sergeant X's nervous breakdown is the main topic in "For Esmé—With Love and Squalor," we do not find out what caused that breakdown. This is because the story skips from a few days before D-Day to a time "several weeks after VE-Day." But we do learn that Sergeant X's regiment fought "from D-Day straight through five campaigns of the war."[10] We also learn that Sergeant X's jeep driver, Corporal Clay, had his picture taken in the Hürtgen Forest "with a Thanksgiving Turkey in each hand."[11] The US Army did indeed ship Thanksgiving turkeys to the soldiers in the Hürtgen Forest.

In part two of "For Esmé," Sergeant X has just returned from a two-week stay at an Army hospital in Frankfurt, Germany. There he has been treated for what the narrator calls a "nervous breakdown" (rather than combat fatigue).

Whatever treatment Sergeant X received at the hospital did not help much because upon his return he still feels as if his mind were about "to dislodge itself and teeter, like insecure luggage on an overhead rack," and when he tries to write, his writing is "almost entirely illegible." He also feels so nauseous most of the time that he keeps a wastebasket handy to vomit into. And Corporal Clay tells him, "the goddam side of your face is jumping all over the place."

It is likely that in describing the aftereffects of Sergeant X's nervous breakdown Salinger was drawing on his own experiences. Salinger shared at least one of Sergeant X's afflictions: the uncontrollable trembling of his hands. In her memoir, *Dream Catcher*, Margaret Salinger reports that she examined the letters that her father wrote during the spring and summer of 1945 and that his handwriting became "something *totally* unrecognizable."[12]

The nervous breakdowns of Sergeant Salinger and Sergeant X illuminate each other. "For Esmé" illustrates the aftereffects of the nervous collapse, the feeling of vertigo, the nausea, the facial tic, and the trembling hands. And Salinger's visit to a concentration camp suggests that his and Sergeant X's nervous breakdowns were triggered by the harrowing experience of becoming Holocaust witnesses.

Salinger's concentration camp experience can also shed light on the suicide of Seymour Glass, the central character in "A Perfect Day for Bananafish" and "Seymour: An Introduction." In the latter story we learn that like Salinger, Seymour Glass was a sergeant in the army, served in Europe, and wound up in Germany at the end of the war. In "A Perfect Day for Bananafish," a psychiatrist says about Seymour that "it was a perfect *crime* the Army released him from the hospital" because there is "a very *great* chance he said—that Seymour may com*pletely* lose control of himself."[13]

No one who has written about the suicide of Seymour Glass has commented on the unusual length of time—almost three years—that he spent in an army hospital. He killed himself on March 18, 1948, and his brother Buddy Glass mentions in "Seymour: An Introduction" that Seymour returned from Germany on a commercial flight "a week or so" before his suicide. That means Seymour did not come home to the United States until almost three years after the end of the war. Buddy also says that Seymour spent "the last three years of his life both in and out of the Army, but mostly in, well in."[14] In short, Seymour's mental illness was so severe that the army psychiatrists did not simply release him with a psychiatric discharge—which is something that Sergeant Salinger was eager to avoid—but decided to keep him "well in."

Seymour's extended stay in an army hospital raises the question of what it was that caused his nervous breakdown and mental illness. Unless we assume that Seymour and Sergeant X are the same person (which some Salinger scholars have done), there is no information in Salinger's fiction about Seymour's war experiences. Seymour may have been a combat infantryman and may have suffered from combat fatigue like Lewis Gardner in "The Magic Foxhole." Or he may have been one of the few survivors of a massacre like the one at Malmedy in Belgium, where the SS killed dozens of American prisoners of war. But since none of this happened to Salinger, it makes more sense to assume that Seymour's nervous breakdown—like Salinger's—was not caused by combat fatigue but was triggered by the gruesome sights and smells of one of the many concentration camps that the US Army discovered in Germany.

When we consider the horrors that Salinger observed at the Kaufering concentration camp, we would assume that in his fiction he would create characters who unequivocally condemn the Nazis and abhor all things German. But Sergeant X and Seymour Glass never show an antagonistic attitude toward Germany and the Nazis. For example, Sergeant X expresses less contempt for the Nazis than for his American fellow soldiers, and he has great sympathy for a Nazi woman he has to arrest. And in "A Perfect Day for Bananafish," Seymour Glass reveals his admiration for German literature when he sends his wife a book of German poems, saying that "the poems happen to be written by the *only great poet of the century*." Because the poems are in German, Seymour tells his wife that she "should've bought a translation or something. Or *learned the language*."[15]

If Sergeant X and Seymour Glass are indeed Holocaust witnesses like Salinger, then their nonjudgmental attitude toward the Nazis is as perplexing as Salinger's. In trying to understand this paradox, I keep coming back to Salinger's nervous breakdown.

Salinger's May 13, 1945, letter to Elizabeth Murray shows that his nervous collapse had a more profound effect on his mind than mere despondency—that it impaired his judgment and his rationality. The letter does not mention his concentration camp experience, but it suggests two additional reasons for his nervous breakdown.

Salinger hints at one of these two additional reasons when he says the war is "a tricky, dreary farce, and how many men are dead." I believe that he is here referring to the many corpses of combat soldiers he saw every time after a battle when he and the other field agents of his CIC detachment had to collect information from abandoned Wehrmacht command posts and from dead German soldiers.

The sights Salinger saw while doing his work are described by Colonel Gerden Johnson, the historian of Salinger's Twelfth Infantry Regiment. Here is what Johnson said about the aftermath of the battle near Longueville in Normandy: "The carnage was frightful and the enemy dead lay in heaps about their shattered vehicles. . . . The next morning it took three two and one-half ton trucks to remove all the German bodies."[16]

But often Salinger saw just as many dead Americans as Germans. For instance, during the battle for Saint-Lô—one of the worst battles Salinger's Twelfth Regiment fought—the number of American casualties was horrific. In that one-week battle, the US Army suffered five thousand casualties including twelve hundred dead.

To face the battlefield carnage, Salinger and the other field agents of his CIC detachment had to develop a mental mechanism that allowed them to cope. This belief of mine is corroborated by the war historian Paul Fussell, himself a veteran of D-Day and of the fighting in Normandy. In his autobiography, *Doing Battle,* Fussell writes:

> Before we'd finished in Europe, we'd seen hundreds of dead bodies, GIs as well as Germans, civilians as well as soldiers, officers as well as enlisted men, together with ample children. We learned that no infantry-man can survive psychologically very long unless he's mastered the principle that the dead don't *know* what they look like. The soldier smiling is *not* smiling, the man whose mouth drips blood doesn't know what he's doing, the man with half his skull blown away and his brain oozing onto the ground thinks he still looks O.K. And the man whose cold eyes stare at you as if expressing a grievance is not doing that. He is elsewhere. The bodies are props on a set, and one must know that their meaning now is that they are props, nothing more.[17]

But unlike Paul Fussell, who did not blank out the horrific images of death but reinterpreted them, Salinger seems to have adopted a coping strategy of avoidance. That is, he seems to have worked hard to avoid thinking of the thousands of corpses he saw while doing his work as a CIC agent, and especially to avoid thinking of the burned bodies he saw and smelled at the Kaufering concentration camp.

The disturbed letter Salinger wrote less than a week after the end of the war points to one more reason for his nervous breakdown. Salinger refers to that reason when he talks about his "own little war." The context of the letter and a comment he made to Hemingway suggest that this is a reference to his adversarial feelings toward the US Army. I believe that the reason why Salinger hated the war and the army was his anger at the military leaders who caused the thousands of unnecessary American casualties at Slapton Sands, Saint-Lô, and the Hürtgen Forest. It seems, then, that the sights and smells of the charred corpses at the Kaufering concentration camp were not the only causes for Salinger's nervous breakdown but only the trigger that set it off.

More important than the causes of Salinger's nervous collapse are its effects on his mind. As his reference to the war as a "tricky, dreary farce" shows, the nervous breakdown impaired his judgment. There is arguably something wrong with the judgment of a World War II soldier who dislikes the US Army more than he does the Nazis and who sees nothing wrong in bringing a German wife home to live with him in the household of his Jewish family. This was more than bad judgment. Salinger's family must have felt that he had undergone a personality change.

A number of studies have established that posttraumatic stress disorder can result in personality changes. One of these studies is titled "Personality Disorders in Treatment-Seeking Combat Veterans with Posttraumatic Stress Disorder." The authors of this study conclude that "chronic war-related PTSD is often accompanied by diffuse, debilitating, enduring impairment in character." This impairment frequently takes the form of an avoidant personality disorder or a borderline personality disorder.[18] Salinger seems to have experienced both.

With Salinger, the more pronounced of the two disorders appears to be the avoidant kind. According to the *Diagnostic and Statistical Manual of Mental Disorders*, one of the essential features of avoidant personality disorder is "hypersensitivity to negative evaluation." Individuals with this disorder "avoid making new friends unless they are certain they will be liked and accepted without criticism. . . . If someone is even slightly disapproving or critical, they may feel extremely hurt." As a result, "these individuals may become relatively isolated."[19] Salinger's decision to stop publishing and to hide from the public in rural New Hampshire can therefore be explained as a result of his hypersensitivity to criticism. His sister, Doris, has confirmed this notion. She said: "Not publishing all these years. What a crazy business. It's because he can't stand any criticism."[20]

In addition to an avoidant personality disorder, Salinger also seems to have been afflicted with a borderline personality disorder. Despite its name, borderline personality disorders do not hover on a borderline between two other psychiatric disorders but have their own unique set of symptoms. According to the *Diagnostic and Statistical Manual of Mental Disorders*, the most prominent symptom of borderline personality disorders is "a pattern of unstable and intense personal relationships characterized by alternating between extremes of idealization and devaluation." Other symptoms are "co-occuring depressive disorders."[21]

Salinger himself has mentioned depression as one of the symptoms of his nervous breakdown. And his relationships with women that Shane Salerno documents in his 2013 book and movie about Salinger show that shifts from idealization to devaluation were a definite pattern in Salinger's attitude toward females. My next chapter deals with Salinger's brief marriage to the German physician Sylvia Welter. That marriage was doomed for several reasons, among them Salinger's personality disorders caused by his posttraumatic stress.

13

Was Salinger's German Wife a Nazi?

For a long time, Salinger scholars knew next to nothing about the European woman Salinger married shortly after the end of World War II. In his book *In Search of J. D. Salinger* (1987), Ian Hamilton claimed that Salinger's European wife was French, that her name was Sylvia, and that she was a doctor, either a psychologist or an osteopath.[1] But in her memoir, *Dream Catcher* (2000), Salinger's daughter, Margaret, asserted that the woman was German and that she had been a minor official in the Nazi Party. Margaret based that assertion on the story "For Esmé—With Love and Squalor" and on the impression the woman made when Salinger brought her home to live with him in the household of his Jewish family.

In part two of "For Esmé," Salinger's alter ego, the CIC agent Sergeant X, is stationed with the Army of Occupation in a small Bavarian town. Shortly after taking up his duties there, Sergeant X arrests the thirty-eight-year-old, unmarried daughter of the family that had been living in the house requisitioned as living quarters for Sergeant X's CIC detachment. He arrests this woman because she had been "a low official in the Nazi Party but high enough by Army Regulations standards to fall into an automatic arrest category." In her memoir, Margaret Salinger says that "sergeant Salinger himself had arrested her. She and Jerry were married by summer's end." Next, Margaret reports that Salinger's family did not get along with Sylvia when he brought her to New York to live with him in his parents' apartment. As a result, "Sylvia went back to Europe for good several months later." Salinger's parents didn't like Sylvia even though she was a brilliant person, "some sort of doctor" who had "accomplished something at a young age." And Salinger's sister, Doris, described Sylvia as looking like Morticia from the TV series *The Addams Family*: "a tall, thin woman with dark hair, pale skin, and blood-red lips and nails." According to Doris, Sylvia was "*very* German" because she had "a sharp incisive way of speaking." Margaret winds up her Sylvia story by quoting her mother, Claire, Salinger's second wife, as saying that "Sylvia hated Jews as much as he [Salinger] hated Nazis" and that he had married her only because she had "bewitched" him.[2]

Margaret Salinger did not know what Sylvia's maiden name was, and without having a last name for her, I found it impossible to verify whether Sylvia had indeed been a Nazi. I wasted a lot of time in Bavarian archives hunting for a low-level Nazi official by the name of Sylvia. But then, on July 24, 2007, a Google alert for the name Salinger directed me to a letter to the editor of a newspaper in North Carolina, the *Hendersonville Times-News*. In that letter, Richard Swift, an acquaintance of Sylvia's, commented on her death, which had occurred on July 16. Swift mentioned that Sylvia was an optician practicing under the name of Sylvie Louise Cary and that her maiden name was Welter: "Sylvie Welter married Jerome David Salinger (born Jan 1, 1919) in Switzerland. . . . They were divorced about five years later as his Jewish parents were not happy that he married a French girl."[3]

Once I had Sylvia's maiden name, it did not take me long to discover that the information in Richard Swift's letter to the editor is as incorrect as some of the things that Margaret Salinger wrote about Sylvia in her memoir. To sort out the conflicting information about Sylvia, I first decided to find out if Sylvia was German or French. In the process of consulting various German archives, I discovered that Sylvia Welter was actually German but claimed to be French when she married Salinger.

Sylvia's father, Ernst Friedrich Welter, was born in Paris and had a German as well as a French passport. Sylvia's mother, Bertha Luise Dépireux, was not French as her maiden name suggests. She was a German citizen, born in Frankfurt am Main. Sylvia was also born in Frankfurt, on April 19, 1919. Her birth certificate lists Sylvia's nationality as German and spells her middle name the German way, as Luise. Her parents moved to Lugano in the Italian-speaking part of Switzerland shortly after Sylvia was born, and they stayed there for almost ten years. In 1929 they moved back to Germany, where Sylvia attended a secondary school for girls in Nuremberg, the Real Gymnasium für Mädchen in the Findelgasse. She graduated in 1938. During the following six years, Sylvia attended the universities of Erlangen, Munich, Prague, Königsberg, and Freiburg before she received her doctorate in medicine from the University of

Jerry and Sylvia Salinger, October 1945 (Welter family photo)

Innsbruck on February 6, 1945. On March 12, 1945, she began to work as a resident at the municipal hospital in the small town of Weißenburg, where Salinger was stationed. When she registered at the Weißenburg *Einwohner Meldeamt* (resident registry), she declared herself to be a citizen of the "German Reich." But when she married Salinger on October 18, 1945, at the *Standesamt* (birth and marriage registry) of the small town of Pappenheim, she listed her nationality as French. However, she still spelled her middle name the German way, as Luise.

Seven months later, on May 10, 1946, Jerry and Sylvia Salinger arrived in New York on the War Shipping Administration freighter *Ethan Allen*. On her immigration form, Sylvia again claimed French citizenship, but she now spelled her middle name the French way, as Louise. Sylvia also listed her occupation as housewife rather than medical doctor. Long after Sylvia's marriage with Salinger had ended, she married another American, moved to the United States, and set up a practice as an ophthalmologist in the town of Hendersonville, North Carolina. But she still claimed to be French and had people call her by the French name of Sylvie.

The deceptions concerning Sylvia's citizenship are easy to understand. First of all, Sylvia could not have married Salinger if she had admitted she was German. The second deception, the one upon entering the United States, seems to have been intended to appease Salinger's Jewish family. But she didn't fool the Salingers. They recognized at once that she wasn't French but German. And the third deception, which lasted the rest of her life, was probably motivated by her fear that Americans would reject her as a former citizen of Nazi Germany. This would not have been an unfounded fear; in the late 1950s, when Sylvia came to settle in the United States, American movies and television shows still depicted most Germans as villains.

The US Army's nonfraternization laws forbade Salinger to marry a German citizen. In February 1945, General Eisenhower's supreme headquarters published a directive that prohibited fraternization between American soldiers and German men, women, or children. On May 16, 1945, the commander of Salinger's Fourth Infantry Division, General Harold W. Blakeley, issued the following order to his troops: "There will be no fraternization between personnel of this command and German officials or population. Violation of existing policies and orders will not be tolerated, and violators will be severely punished."[4] US Army historian Earl Ziemke reports that violation of the nonfraternization order "could result in as much as six months' confinement and two-thirds loss of pay."[5] The nonfraternization order was gradually relaxed as the year 1945 wore on, but the law prohibiting American soldiers from marrying German women remained in force until December 11, 1946.[6]

Salinger could marry Sylvia only if he could prove that she was not German. Since she spoke fluent French, it was an obvious choice to pass her off as a citizen of France. This was not difficult for Salinger because in 1945 it was one of the tasks of the CIC to issue new identification papers to thousands of displaced persons—that is, people whom the Nazis had deported from their countries to do slave labor in Germany. So Salinger simply forged a French passport for Sylvia. And indeed, Kenneth Slawenski reports in his Salinger biography that "Sylvia's 'French' passport was found among her belongings upon her death."[7]

Margaret Salinger was right when she said that Sylvia was German, but she made two incorrect assumptions. Both assumptions are based on her belief that Sylvia is the real-life model for the Nazi woman in "For Esmé—With Love and Squalor." Treating the story as autobiography, Margaret assumed first of all that her father had arrested Sylvia when his CIC detachment took over her parents' house as living quarters. Second, Margaret assumed that Sylvia was a low-level official in the Nazi Party.

If Salinger had really arrested Sylvia, then her name would show up in military archives. In the Special Operations Reports of the Fourth Infantry Division for April and May of 1945, I found lists of all individuals that Salinger's CIC detachment arrested. Among the more than two hundred people listed, there is no one by the name of Sylvia Luise Welter.

To find out whether Sylvia had been a low-level official in the Nazi Party or in the Reichsärztekammer (League of Nazi Physicians), I contacted the Bundesarchiv, the German National Archives in Berlin. A Matthias Meissner e-mailed me that "in the personnel files of the Bundesarchiv no indication was found of membership in the two organizations"—the Nazi Party and League of Nazi Physicians. In short, we can be sure that Sylvia was neither a minor official nor even a member of the Nazi Party.

Since Sylvia did not serve as the inspiration for the Nazi woman in "For Esmé," I wondered what real-life person did. When I visited the Weißenburg town archive, I found out that the private home that the US Army had requisitioned as quarters for the CIC agents had belonged to a family by the name of Müller. They had a twenty-three-year-old daughter, Anneliese, but this Anneliese Müller was not a member of the Nazi Party. Next I inquired after the family that owned the Villa Oberwegner, the mansion that had been requisitioned for the offices of Salinger's CIC detachment. It belonged to Adam Wohlleben, the owner of the local lumber mill. Neither he nor his wife were members of the Nazi Party. But his brother Rudolf Wohlleben was a low-level official in the Party and an *Unterscharführer* (noncommissioned officer) in the SS. He was arrested when the offices of Salinger's CIC detachment were moved into the Villa Oberwegner.

So the model for the Nazi woman in "For Esmé—With Love and Squalor" was not a single person. Instead, Salinger seems to have created that fictional character as a composite of two people, Anneliese Müller, the daughter of the family in whose home Salinger and his CIC colleagues were quartered, and Rudolf Wohlleben, the brother of Adam Wohlleben, in whose home the CIC offices were located.

Since Salinger did not meet Sylvia by arresting her, as his daughter, Margaret, claims, I was curious as to how the two of them met. At the Weißenburg town archive I found out that the place where Sylvia lived was an apartment in the Kehler Weg 10a (now Schiller Straße 1). To get from her apartment to the hospital where she worked, she had to walk past the house in the Dr. Dörfler Straße 20, where Salinger and his CIC colleagues had their quarters. I assumed that Salinger often saw the pretty young woman walk by and eventually started a conversation with her. But I was mistaken.

The question of where and when Salinger met Sylvia is answered in an unpublished interview that the journalist Jan Stephan conducted with Sylvia's second-cousins Bernhard and Günter Horn. They reported that Sylvia's sister Alice had told them it was she who brought Sylvia and Salinger together, and that this happened toward the end of May 1945, less than a month after the end of the war. Because Alice spoke English quite well, she had found employment at the American military hospital in Nuremberg. While Alice was having a bag lunch in the hospital's garden, she had a conversation with a tall, dark-haired American sergeant who mentioned that he was stationed in the town of Weißenburg. Alice told him that her sister and mother happened to live in that town and that she was hoping to visit them very soon. The American soldier offered to give her a ride, and Alice happily accepted. That sergeant was J. D. Salinger.

Salinger met Sylvia when he dropped Alice off in Weißenburg. Alice reported that Salinger and Sylvia immediately "struck up a lively conversation." One thing led to another, and five months later the two were married. Every time Alice told that story, she ended with the comment that Sylvia never forgave her, as long she lived, for having brought her and Salinger together.

Margaret Salinger's assumption that Sylvia was the real life model for the Nazi woman in "For Esmé" is as far off the mark as her assertion that the reason for the break-up of her father's first marriage was Sylvia's alleged anti-Semitism. If Sylvia really hated Jews, then why would she have married Salinger? There are three other reasons why the marriage broke up.

Even though Sylvia had not been a member of the Nazi Party, she would have been repugnant to the Salinger family just because she was German. After all, the family was Jewish. Also, in May 1946, when Salinger brought Sylvia back to the United States, the Nuremberg war crimes trials were still going on, and the horrific images of piles of corpses at the Dachau, Buchenwald, and Bergen-Belsen concentration camps were still fresh in the minds of most Americans, and especially in the minds of Jewish Americans.

But the inability of Salinger's family to accept his choice of a German wife was only one of three reasons for the break-up of the marriage. The second reason was that Salinger began to develop negative feelings toward Sylvia early on in their marriage. This is suggested in a strange letter from Gunzenhausen that Salinger wrote to his old friend Elizabeth Murray on December 30, 1945. In that letter Salinger not only indulged in what to him must have seemed like hilarious fictions but he also displayed passive aggressive tendencies toward Sylvia.

Salinger began the letter by asserting "we are very happy" and that Sylvia was "so fine, intelligent, and beautiful." After a few comments about the stories he had coming out in American magazines—among them "The Stranger" and the Holden Caulfield story "I'm Crazy"—Salinger fibbed about the place where he and Sylvia were living.

Salinger said that they "live alone in a perfect little house filled with coal and canned peanuts." But in reality they lived in a large house called the Villa Schmidt. Also they did not live alone there because the offices of his CIC detachment had been moved to that building from Weißenburg. Also the Salingers employed a cook and a woman who did their laundry.

Salinger topped these untruths with fiction about his and Sylvia's Christmas celebration. When he said they had a Christmas tree and a big turkey provided by the US Army, that rings true. But then he claimed that at the stroke of midnight, he and Sylvia "threw rotten eggs at each other—a custom of the people here." Because I was born in nearby Nuremberg, I can testify that there is no such custom in that part of Germany.

The untruths and the subliminal hostility in the letter continue in the next to last paragraph, when Salinger said that at present, Sylvia had her hair in pigtails and that "over her shoulders is a large, ungainly mail sack." Then he offered the bogus explanation that "she was a letter carrier before we were married and is very sentimental."[8]

In this letter, Salinger comes across as being almost as unstable as in the May 13 letter he wrote immediately after his nervous breakdown. He began by asserting how happy he was with Sylvia and how "fine, intelligent, and beautiful" she was. But then he described her in less than flattering terms as wearing an "ungainly mail sack" and having been a "letter carrier" before they met. These contradictory statements suggest that he was still emotionally unbalanced as a result of his posttraumatic stress. It must have been hard for Sylvia to cope with his mood swings.

Sylvia's sister Alice confirmed that Jerry and Sylvia had marital problems early on. During Stephan's interview with Sylvia's cousins, Bernhard Horn remembered Alice telling him in March 1946 that the young couple's marriage was none too happy. At that time Jerry and Sylvia Salinger were living in two back rooms of the large apartment of Sylvia's parents in Nuremberg. When Bernhard was released from an American prisoner of war camp and made his first postwar visit to the Welters, Alice took him aside and warned him that Sylvia and her American husband were "constantly fighting." Part of their problem was apparently that Sylvia's family was unhappy about her marriage to an American.

Bernhard Horn was also unhappy about Sylvia's marriage to Salinger because he had a crush on Sylvia before he was drafted into the Wehrmacht in 1942. When Bernhard met Salinger at the Welters' apartment, he didn't hide his feelings. He told Salinger that he had been severely mistreated as a prisoner of war and that he intensely disliked all Americans. Despite Bernhard's bluntness, Salinger remained friendly and even gave him a present, a copy of Somerset Maugham's novel *The Razor's Edge*. That novel begins with an epigraph from the *Katha Upanishad* and contains an explanation of Vedanta Hinduism that is even more detailed than the one Salinger later developed in the story "Teddy" (1953).

Salinger's gift of the Somerset Maugham novel did not diminish Bernhard Horn's dismay about Sylvia marrying Salinger. But his dismay and that of Sylvia's parents was nothing compared to the dismay of Salinger's parents. Although their unhappiness about Salinger marrying a German woman is more understandable than the Welter family's unhappiness about Sylvia marrying an American, there seems to have been a good deal more cruelty involved on the part of the Salingers. Hildegard Mayer, a school friend of Sylvia's, was interviewed by the journalist Bernd Noack, and she reported that Sylvia told her "she never cried as much as she did at that time. And one day an airline ticket was lying on the breakfast table. They wanted to get rid of her."[9]

Margaret Salinger suggests the reason her father and Sylvia's marriage broke up was that Sylvia hated Jews. But Salinger did not mention Sylvia's alleged anti-Semitism in two letters in which he told friends about the break-up.

In the letter to his CIC buddy Paul Fitzgerald, Salinger said very little about Sylvia and only explained that "almost from the beginning, we were desperately unsuited to, and unhappy with, each other."[10] But in the letter to his confidante Elizabeth Murray, Salinger gave a more detailed explanation. He said that the marriage was "a failure — or the participants were" and that he and Sylvia "brought each other the most violent kind of unhappiness." He then explained what the reason for his unhappiness was: "I didn't write the whole time I was married."[11] People who knew Salinger in the army report that he was used to writing every day. For him, not being able to write would have been almost as bad as not being able to breathe. For instance, fellow CIC agent Jack Altaras reports: "He lugged that little portable typewriter all over Europe. I can remember him down under a table pecking away while we were under attack near a front."[12]

On January 26, 1949, a decree of the Family Court of Queens County, New York, annulled Salinger's marriage to Sylvia Welter. This happened at Salinger's request. He accused Sylvia of "deception" and of having married him under "false pretenses." The annulment decree does not state what the nature of the deception was.

I had assumed that in order to extricate himself from the unhappy marriage, Salinger might have asserted that Sylvia deceived him by claiming to be French when she was really German. But the David Shields and Shane Salerno biography, *Salinger*, quotes a college friend of Salinger's, Leila Hadley Luce, saying that Salinger had told her he had the marriage annulled after "he found out some disturbing things about what she did in the war, specifically with the Gestapo."[13]

The Gestapo was the Nazis' *Geheime Staatspolizei* (secret state police). In an article titled "Omniscient, Omnipotent, and Omnipresent? Gestapo, Society, and Resistance," the German historians Klaus-Michael Mallmann and Gerhard Paul show that the Gestapo was not as formidable an organization as is commonly assumed. Their data show that the Gestapo was so poorly funded that it did not have the means to conduct its own investigations but relied mostly on denunciations of individuals and groups by private informers. For example, the Gestapo district office in Nuremberg consisted of only six agents, who were "responsible for the entire area of Northern Bavaria." But that Gestapo office "had at its disposal in 1943–4 somewhat more than eighty to 100 informers, who reported on anti-regime attitudes, efforts and incidents that came to their attention."[14] Because the Gestapo offices in most German cities destroyed their files during the last days of the war, there is no documented proof that Sylvia had been working for the Gestapo.

If Sylvia had really been a Gestapo informer, I would have run across some information or at least some hints to that effect in one of the Sylvia files in the German archives I visited. The Gestapo is mentioned in only one file, the one in the Nuremberg city archive, and the reason for the reference to the Gestapo is that Sylvia lost her passport in Switzerland, and the German consulate in Geneva needed Gestapo approval to issue her a new one.

But I did run across something strange in Sylvia's biography that might suggest there could have been a Gestapo connection after all. It is odd that between 1939 and 1945 Sylvia was enrolled at six different universities. Before World War II, most German students switched universities at least once to widen their horizons. But it was highly unusual for anyone to attend six different universities. Could it be possible that the Gestapo enrolled Sylvia at six universities to spy on anti-Nazi student organizations? Between 1942 and 1943, the Gestapo arrested and executed many leaders of this movement, the most prominent being Hans and Sophie Scholl, who headed the Munich student resistance group called the White Rose.

Still, there are two reasons it is unlikely that Sylvia worked for the Gestapo. One is that she does not fit any one of the several profiles of typical Gestapo informers developed by the historian Walter Otto Weyrauch in his study "Gestapo Informants: Facts and Theory of Undercover Operations."[15] A second reason is that people who knew Sylvia find it impossible to believe that she was a Gestapo informer. Sylvia's school friend Hildegard Mayer is sure that Sylvia "had no truck with the Regime. She wasn't even in the BDM."[16] Mayer here refers to the Bund Deutscher Mädel (Federation of German Girls), a kind of Nazi Girls Scouts that all German girls were expected to belong to. Also, Günter Horn, one of Sylvia's two cousins, wrote me a letter in response to a rumor that Sylvia had been a Nazi militant and that she had tried to subvert Salinger's work as a special agent for the CIC. Horn was in contact with Sylvia until shortly before her death, and he assured me that "Sylvia was no kind of Nazi whatsoever."[17]

Since Sylvia was not a low-level official in the Nazi Party nor even a Party member and since there is no documented proof that she had anything to do with the Gestapo, the answer to the question of whether Salinger's German wife was a Nazi has to be no.

Although much of what Margaret Salinger said about her father's German wife and about the breakup of the marriage must be dismissed, her comments about the aftermath of the breakup sound true enough. Margaret mentions that her father conceded that Sylvia was "an extraordinary woman" and that their marriage "was extremely intense, both physically and emotionally." Still he occasionally referred to Sylvia by the unkind name of "Saliva." Margaret also reports that sometime in the early 1970s she witnessed her father tearing up a letter from Sylvia without reading it. When Margaret asked him why he tore up that letter, Salinger said that "when he was finished with a person, he was through with them."[18]

14

Half-Heartedly Hunting Nazis
after the War

After the end of the war, the nature of Salinger's work for the CIC changed. He no longer had to deal with Nazi spies and saboteurs. His job was now to round up former members of the SS, Nazi officials, and other members of the Nazi Party who had gone into hiding in order to escape their responsibility for crimes they had committed on behalf of the Party. After Salinger was discharged from the US Army, he signed up for a six-month stint as a special investigator for the CIC, and he continued doing essentially the same job he had been doing while still in the army—namely tracking down and arresting Nazis.

Finding Nazis who had gone into hiding was not as difficult as it may seem because under the Nazi system of government, a person could not be the mayor or the police chief of a town or village, and not even a school principal, without being a member of the Nazi Party. And the CIC had lists of all town and village officials, as well as lists of functionaries in such Nazi organizations as the SS, the Gestapo, and the Abwehr (Nazi counterintelligence).

The diary of Salinger's CIC buddy Paul Fitzgerald illustrates what kinds of Nazis they were hunting. For instance, in a village by the name of Pleinfeld, population 1,636, Salinger's CIC detachment was looking particularly for what Fitzgerald called "rabid Nazis." Among them were Alois Haindel, the *Orts-gruppenleiter* (the local Nazi Party chief), Anna Schreck, an agent of the SD (*Sicherheitsdienst*, the security police of the SS), and Karl Hensold, a slave labor camp commander who had mistreated the Russian prisoners of that camp.[1]

Two stories that reflect Salinger's postwar task of hunting down former Nazis are "A Girl I Knew" and "For Esmé—With Love and Squalor." Both stories suggest that Salinger was not enthusiastic about arresting Nazis. And two of his letters from 1945 show that he came to see his Nazi hunting as a joke.

By November 1945, when Salinger began his work as a special investigator, the chief responsibility of the CIC had become the denazification program. The program was created by the Allied Control Council even before Germany and Austria were completely occupied. The purpose of denazification was to remove all Nazi officials from positions of influence and to punish all former members of the Nazi Party for having supported an evil regime. The basic assumption behind denazification was that all Germans and Austrians were Nazis unless they could provide proof to the contrary. To determine the degree of their guilt, the Allies agreed to make all Germans and Austrians who were over eighteen years old fill out a questionnaire, the infamous *Fragebogen*. The questionnaire consisted of 131 questions that asked respondents to indicate whether they belonged to the Nazi Party, the SA, the SS, or one of forty-nine other organizations affiliated directly or indirectly with the Party.[2] These organizations ranged all the way from the Physicians' League and the Teachers' Union down to the Confederation of German Mothers and the Hitler Youth. This created a huge logistical problem because most Germans and Austrians belonged to one or more such organizations.

After respondents filled out the *Fragebogen*, they had to appear before a denazification court (later called the *Spruchkammer*). That court assigned respondents to one of five categories according to their degree of guilt. In his book *Exorcising Hitler: The Occupation and Denazification of Germany*, Frederick Taylor translates those categories as follows:

V. Exonerated, or non-incriminated persons (*Entlastete*)

IV. Followers, or Fellow Travellers (*Mitläufer*)

III. Less Incriminated (*Minderbelastete*)

II. Activists, Militants, and Profiteers, or Incriminated Persons (*Belastete*)

I. Major Offenders (*Hauptschuldige*)

The sanctions imposed by the denazification courts ranged from fines to restrictions on employment and travel, and in some cases capital punishment.[3]

For instance, my father, Karl Alsen, had been a *Rottenführer* (platoon leader) of the paramilitary SA from 1933 to 1935 and a member of the Nazi Party from 1937 to 1938. In a remarkably lenient judgment, he was classified as a *Mitläufer* and got away with no other sanctions than a fine of 1,000 Reichsmarks. But because he could not pay that fine, he had to serve on a highway repair crew for twenty-five days, earning forty Reichsmarks per day.

The people in the category below the "Followers," the "Less Incriminated," also had to pay fines, and they were barred from public office and placed on probation for two to three years. The more serious "Activists, Militants, and Profiteers" were sentenced to prison terms and hard labor and were barred from all but the most menial jobs. And the "Major Offenders" could expect long prison terms and in some cases even capital punishment by hanging.

The "Major Offenders" were such well-known figures that the CIC was able to apprehend most of them without too much difficulty. But many lower-level Nazis who knew that they would probably be classified as "Activists, Militants, or Profiteers" did not fill out the *Fragebogen* and instead went into hiding. And it was these small-time Nazis that it was Salinger's job to arrest.

In tracking these Nazis down, so the authors of the *History of the Counter Intelligence Corps* explain, CIC agents relied heavily on Germans informing on their neighbors: "The majority of informants who wished to expose former Nazis went directly to the German police, although some denouncers came to the CIC." The German police also helped CIC agents with the apprehension of fugitive Nazis: "In the actual arrest procedure, CIC agents generally accompanied the German police. Suspects were apprehended at their homes, and H-hour was generally designated as 0300 hours, a time at which the individual was most likely to be in bed, surprised, and unprepared to offer resistance or attempt to escape."[4]

After Salinger had arrested a Nazi, his CIC detachment would send that person to an internment camp. Some detainees spent several years in such camps before their cases were heard. My father was not put into an internment camp because he had turned himself in to a denazification court, but he was not denazified until February 1947.

Originally OMGUS (the Office of the Military Government, United States) tried to accomplish the task of denazification through special courts staffed by the divisional civilian affairs detachments of the US Army. But these courts could not keep up with the staggering number of former Nazis waiting for their trials. By March 1946, the military government's judge advocate estimated that the number of persons in internment camps was 100,000, but the Denazification Policy Board believed that "the number to be tried might well be 500,000."[5] The military governor of the American Zone of Occupation, General Lucius Clay, reported to Washington that "even if the War Department were to send him 10,000 Americans for the purpose, he could not denazify the US Zone."[6]

OMGUS resolved the dilemma by turning the denazification program over to the Germans. This happened during a ceremony at Munich City Hall

Skoda car like the one Salinger went Nazi hunting in (Skoda Muzeum, Czech Republic)

on March 5, 1946. But the German denazification courts, or *Spruchkammern*, immediately developed a reputation for whitewashing former Nazis officials. This must have made Salinger realize that denazification was not working.

There are two letters in which Salinger pokes fun at his work as a Nazi hunter. One is his July 1945 letter to Ernest Hemingway. In that letter Salinger said, "there are very few arrests left to be made in our section. We're now picking up children under ten if their attitudes are snotty."[7] And in his December 1945 letter to Elizabeth Murray, Salinger reported that he went Nazi hunting in "a new and very snappy two-seater Skoda which we drive over the roads at a rate of five thousand miles an hour" and that "a dog, a big black one named Benny . . . rides on the running board, pointing out Nazis for me to arrest."[8]

Salinger's stories "A Girl I Knew" and "For Esmé—With Love and Squalor" suggest still another reason why he was less than enthusiastic about his Nazi hunting. Those two stories demonstrate a nonjudgmental and even sympathetic attitude toward his Nazis characters while depicting American soldiers as unlikeable.

Part two of "A Girl I Knew" takes place in Germany shortly after the end of the war. The narrator of the story—who identifies himself only as John—tells us that during the war in Europe he "had an intelligence job with a regiment of an infantry division" and that his work "called for a lot of conversation with civilians and Wehrmacht prisoners." This describes exactly what Salinger's own job was. The purpose of the interrogations that John and Salinger conducted was to ferret out Nazis officials and members of the SS who were posing as civilians or common soldiers. Like Salinger, the narrator, John, was a staff sergeant.

During one interrogation, John discovers that a soldier claiming to be a sergeant of the regular German army was actually a member of the SS. Here is the passage about this Nazi:

> Another *Wiener* [Viennese], an *unteroffizier* [buck sergeant] standing at strict attention, told me what terrible things had been done to the Jews in Vienna. As I had rarely, if ever, seen a man with a face quite so noble and full of vicarious suffering as this *unteroffizier*'s was, just for the devil of it I had him roll up his left sleeve. Close to his armpit he had the tattooed blood-type marks of an old SS-man. I stopped asking personal questions after that.[9]

After John unmasks the man's noble posture and his pretension of vicarious suffering, he does not want to investigate his wartime record. But this Austrian Nazi might have been a guard at a concentration camp, or he might have been a member of the Waffen-SS, which was responsible for a number of major massacres, such as the one at Oradour, France, where they wiped out an entire village, killing 642 men, women, and children. When John explains that after interrogating the SS sergeant, he did not want to ask "personal questions" of Nazis anymore, he reveals a head-in-the-sand attitude similar to Salinger's own.

The narrator in "For Esmé," Sergeant X, does not show the same detached, nonjudgmental attitude toward a Nazi he arrests. He shows outright sympathy. When Sergeant X arrests a woman who was "a low official in the Nazi Party," he finds in her possession a book by Nazi propaganda minister Joseph Goebbels titled *Die Zeit Ohne Beispiel* [The Time without Equal].

The fact that the woman owned a book by one of the most evil top Nazis should have predisposed Sergeant X to treat the woman with the utmost contempt. Instead he winds up feeling empathy for her. This happens when he discovers a brief inscription on the flyleaf of the Goebbels book: "Written in ink, in German, in a small hopelessly sincere handwriting, were the words, 'Dear God, life is hell.'" Sergeant X is stunned by this inscription. Here is his reaction: "Nothing led up to or away from it. Alone on the page, and in the sickly stillness of the room, the words seemed to have the stature of an uncontestable, even classic indictment." Sergeant X stares at the inscription for a while, and Salinger says that he "was trying against heavy odds, not to be taken in." The heavy odds, of course, are that the woman might have been a former admirer of Goebbels. But Sergeant X can't help being taken in by the Nazi woman's sincerity, despair, and self-hatred.

And so Sergeant X puts a literary spin on the woman's comment that life in Nazi Germany was hell. He picks up a pencil and tries to write under the woman's inscription a quotation from Dostoyevsky, "Fathers, and teachers, I ponder 'What is hell?' I maintain that it is the suffering of being unable to love." Then, when he starts to write Dostoyevsky's name after the quotation, he notices that his writing is illegible because his hand is shaking too much.

Salinger's nonjudgmental attitude toward the Nazis in "A Girl I Knew" and "For Esmé" is surprising when we realize that these two stories were published in 1948 and 1950, only three and five years, respectively, after the defeat of Nazi Germany. At that time, few Americans were as willing to forget and forgive. Even when I first came to the United States in 1962—seventeen years after the end of World War II—I encountered a number of Americans who would not continue to talk to me after they found out I was German. Ten years later the Holocaust still determined the attitudes that many Americans had toward Germans and Germany. Sometime during the 1970s, a Jewish colleague of mine reproached another colleague—also Jewish—for buying a Volkswagen, asking him why he bought an "Auschwitz Wagen." So Salinger's going as easy as he does on the Nazis in his 1948 and 1950 stories is astonishing.

One reason Salinger was only half-hearted in his hunt for fugitive Nazis may have been that he found the low-level Nazis officials he tracked down to be no more despicable than the worst of his fellow soldiers in the US Army. Compared to his portrayal of the Nazis in "A Girl I Knew" and "For Esmé," his depiction of the American soldiers in those two stories is definitely more negative.

In part one of "For Esmé," Salinger has a young English girl tell Sergeant X that most of the American soldiers stationed in England before the D-Day invasion "act like animals" and that one of them even threw a whiskey bottle through the window of her aunt's house. In part two of the story, Salinger paints a portrait of one of those "animals."[10]

Corporal Clay, Sergeant X's jeep driver, is one of the most obnoxious characters in all of Salinger's fiction, and I think Salinger wants us to see him as representing a sizeable element in the US Army. Above all, Corporal Clay regards the war as a great opportunity to show others what a hero he is. Even after peace breaks out, he still drives his jeep around "combat-style, with the windshield down on the hood." He wants to demonstrate to the thousands of new troops in Germany "that not by a long shot was he some new son of a bitch in the E.T.O. [European Theater of Operations]."

To impress the newly arrived troops, Clay always wears all of his medals and then some. For instance, he "was wearing the Infantry Men's Badge," which, Salinger says, "he technically was not authorized to wear." After all, Clay was with the CIC and not with a combat unit. In addition he wears "the European Theater ribbon with five bronze battle stars . . . instead of a lone silver one, which was the equivalent of five bronze ones." Plus Clay wears "the pre–Pearl Harbor service ribbon." Obviously, Clay decorates himself like that to be able to lord it over other soldiers.

Two even more detestable traits of Clay's personality—his cruelty and lack of compassion—become apparent in the story of his shooting a cat. Here is Clay's account of the cat-shooting incident: "'Remember that time I and you drove into Valognes, and we got shelled for about two goddam hours, and that goddam cat I shot that jumped on the hood of the jeep when we were layin' in that hole'?" Clay reported that incident to his girlfriend, Loretta, who is a psychology major in college. And her response was this: "She says that I was temporarily insane." But when Clay writes to Loretta and tells her that Sergeant X had a nervous breakdown, "she says nobody gets a nervous breakdown from the war and all. She says you probably were unstable like, your whole goddam life."

So all this doesn't make Clay worse than an SS sergeant, but the behavior of people like Clay and the soldiers who throw whiskey bottles through civilians' windows in England was one reason that Salinger was more antagonistic toward the US Army than toward the Nazis.

In "A Girl I Knew," Salinger created two additional unsympathetic American soldiers, a staff sergeant and a colonel. We learn about these two from the narrator, the CIC agent named John. When John is sent to deliver military papers from Nuremberg to Vienna, he uses that opportunity to make inquiries about a Jewish girl named Leah and her family, whom he had known before the war. After he learns that they all died in the Buchenwald concentration camp, he decides to revisit the building in Vienna where he and Leah's family used to live.

John finds that the US Army has turned the building into living quarters for field grade officers. It is there that Salinger draws the vignettes of two unsympathetic US Army types: "A red-haired staff sergeant was sitting at an Army desk on the first landing, cleaning his fingernails. He looked up, and, as I didn't outrank him, gave me that long Army look that holds no interest or curiosity at all."[11] John asks the sergeant for permission to go up to the second floor for just a minute, and he explains that he used to live there before the war. But the sergeant tells him, "This here's officers' quarters, Mac." And he adds, "I ain't lettin' nobody go upstairs unless they belong there. I don't give a damn if it's Eisenhower himself."

Then the sergeant gets a phone call from a colonel who asks him about the preparations for a party that evening, and the sergeant is all "Yes Sir, Colonel, Sir," and tells the colonel that "the three piece orchestra will be placed on the balcony" and that "the champagne is being put on ice right this minute."

When the sergeant hangs up, John repeats his request to visit his old room in the building, and the sergeant asks, "What's the big deal anyhow, up there?" "No big deal," John replies, "I just want to go up to the second floor and take a look at the balcony. I used to know a girl who lived in the balcony apartment." When the sergeant asks where that girl is now, John tells him she is dead: "She and her family were burned to death in an incinerator, I'm told." To this, the sergeant replies without a shred of compassion: "Yeah? What was she, a Jew or something?" But John repeats his request to be allowed to go upstairs, and the sergeant reluctantly says, "O.K. Make it snappy."

John enters his old apartment and finds nothing in the room as it was in 1936; instead there are now three military bunks with clothes hanging from them. But he looks out the window and sees "the balcony where Leah once had stood." As John is about to leave the building, the sergeant asks him what the right way is to chill champagne, "lay it on its side or stand it up." In this last section of "A Girl I Knew," Salinger shows another reason he didn't like the army. While he, Salinger, was supposed to bring fugitive Nazis to justice, army types like the officious and insensitive sergeant and the party-minded colonel did not care about the the genocide the Nazis had committed.

What must have also irked Salinger about his job as Nazi hunter was the double standard that the higher-ups in the army used when dealing with former Nazis. That double standard became evident when he US Army's Joint Intelligence Objectives Agency set in motion Operation Paperclip. To implement that project, the CIC was given orders to round up as many German scientists and engineers as possible—no matter if they were Nazis or not—so they could be moved to the United States before the Russians got hold of them. The most famous of those was Wernher von Braun.

The US military government of Germany had submitted a CIC report on Braun to the agency responsible for Operation Paperclip. That report stated that "Braun was considered an ardent Nazi and a security threat to the United States. His record indicated that he had been a major in the SS—having joined the SS at the personal behest of SS chief Heinrich Himmler in 1940—and a Nazi Party member since 1937."[12]

Braun was the principal designer of the V-2 ballistic missile that the Nazis used to devastate London, and he relied on slave labor to mass-produce that rocket in the underground factory at Nordhausen. The slave labor came from the nearby concentration camp Mittelbau-Dora. When this camp was liberated, it became known that "some 20,000 died at Dora, from illness, beatings, hangings and intolerable working conditions."[13] But the movers and shakers of Operation Paperclip swept those facts under the carpet.

President Truman had approved Project Paperclip under the condition that no German scientist or engineer be brought to the United States who had "been a member of the Nazi Party and more than a nominal participant in its activities, or an active supporter of Nazism or militarism."[14] The US Army's Joint Intelligence Objectives Agency falsified the political and employment records of Braun and his team of engineers so they could continue their work on ballistic missiles for the United States. In short, the US Army deliberately hoodwinked the president.

While the Army resettled Braun and over fifteen hundred other white-washed Nazis in the United States to do weapons research, Salinger was expected to track down lesser Nazis in Germany so they could be denazified. This double standard must have reinforced Salinger's negative opinion of the US Army leadership and confirmed his opinion that his job as a Nazi hunter was a ridiculous waste of time.

15

American Bastards and
Nazi Bastards

The great change that occurred in Salinger's attitude toward the Nazis is most apparent when we compare what he says about them in "Last Day of the Last Furlough" (1944) and in *The Catcher in the Rye* (1951). In "Last Day," Salinger's central character, Sergeant Babe Gladwaller, says that he believes in killing Nazis, but in *The Catcher in the Rye*, Holden Caulfield's brother D. B. says that if he had been forced to shoot anybody during the war he wouldn't have known whether to shoot Nazis or "bastards" in the US Army.

Like Salinger, D. B. Caulfield was not a combat soldier; like Salinger, he landed on D-Day; and like Salinger, he did not like the army. In fact, his brother Holden says that D. B. "hated the Army worse than the war." Holden explains: "He didn't get wounded or anything and he didn't have to shoot anybody. All he had to do was drive some cowboy general around all day in a command car. He once told Allie and I that if he'd had to shoot anybody, he wouldn't've known which direction to shoot in. He said the Army was practically as full of bastards as the Nazis were."[1]

While fictional characters don't necessarily speak for their authors, Salinger has made statements suggesting that he shares D. B.'s opinions. Holden's comment that D. B. hated the army worse than the war recalls Hemingway's report that Salinger "hated the Army and the war," and D. B.'s comparison of the bastards in the US Army and among the Nazis recalls the letter in which Salinger wrote about his "own little war" against the army and confessed that his most casual thoughts about the Army were "edgy with treason."

Salinger has given us portraits of US Army personnel that include common soldiers as well as officers, but the bastards D. B. Caulfield refers to would be mostly the higher-ups, in particular the generals. But unlike D. B., Salinger wasn't around generals every day. This is why in his fiction Salinger mentions only two generals, one in the story "Blue Melody" and one in *The Catcher in the Rye*. Both references are brief but biting.

About the general in "Blue Melody," the narrator of the story says that he "seldom stepped into his command car without wearing a Luger [pistol] and a photographer, one on each side" and that he liked to write "crisp, quotable little go-to-hell notes to the enemy" when the Wehrmacht had surrounded his troops.[2] Salinger gave this fictional general the traits of two real life generals. One of them is General Anthony McAuliffe; the other is General George Patton.

General McAuliffe became famous for his response to the Germans when they had surrounded the 101st Airborne Division in the town of Bastogne, Belgium. McAuliffe was acting commander of the division while General Maxwell Taylor was absent. When the commander of the German troops asked McAuliffe to surrender, his reply consisted of only one word: "Nuts." One of McAuliffe's aides had to explain to the Germans that "Nuts to you" means, "Go to hell."[3]

I don't think Salinger felt contempt for McAuliffe, and I don't think Salinger believed that McAuliffe should have surrendered. But Salinger's dislike of Hemingway's macho posturing suggests that he must have disliked the bravado of McAuliffe's response. This bravado could have led to the annihilation of the 101st Airborne Division. But disaster was averted when the 101st Airborne was rescued by one of Patton's armored divisions.

The other general to whom Salinger alludes in "Blue Melody" is Patton, who loved publicity and always wore a holster with a couple of ivory-handled revolvers (not a German Luger as Salinger's fictional general did). The general in *The Catcher in the Rye* whom D. B. drives around in a command car is also reminiscent of Patton because D. B. refers to him as a "cowboy general."

Patton was a brilliant strategist. According to the German general Erwin Rommel, who was his adversary in Africa, Patton was the best general the US Army had. But Patton held some very objectionable opinions. Even though he had been sickened by the piles of emaciated corpses he saw during his visit of the Ohrdruf concentration camp, a subcamp of Buchenwald, Patton wrote to his wife on a different occasion that the Germans are "the only decent people left in Europe" who could help America contain the power of the Soviets. He also felt that denazification was wrong because it was "silly to get rid of the most intelligent people in Germany."

Conversely, Patton wrote in one diary entry that he considered Jewish people to be "lower than animals." And in another diary entry, he said that the "Jewish type of DP [displaced person] is, in the majority of cases, a sub-human species without any of the cultural and social refinements of our time."[4] While the *New York Times* accused Patton of being "pro-Nazi," only Patton's wife and some of his close associates were aware of his anti-Semitism.

Even though Salinger could not have been aware of Patton's contempt for the Jews, he still had a good reason to dislike him. Having suffered a nervous breakdown himself, Salinger must have been well aware of the news stories about Patton slapping two soldiers in army hospitals who suffered from battle fatigue. Patton was intolerant of what he considered the weakness of those soldiers, and he published the following proclamation to his troops on August 5, 1943: "Such men are cowards who bring discredit on the army and disgrace to their comrades whom they heartlessly leave to endure the dangers of battle while they themselves use the hospitals as a mere escape."[5]

Salinger's negative statements about the two fictional generals in "Blue Melody" and *The Catcher in the Rye* confirm that Salinger had no respect for the leadership of the American war effort. After all, he had witnessed three military disasters that were caused by the incompetence of an admiral and the arrogance of two generals.

To reprise these disasters: The first occurred during a training exercise at Slapton Sands in England, where the slipshod planning of Rear Admiral Donald P. Moon resulted in the deaths of 749 American soldiers. The second disaster occurred during the US Air Force's bombing of American troops near Saint-Lô in Normandy, where General Omar Bradley's willingness to accept American casualties resulted in 621 GIs being wounded and 136 killed. The third disaster was the ill-conceived Battle of the Hürtgen Forest in Germany, where General Leonard Gerow's unfamiliarity with the rugged terrain and his unwillingness to listen to field commanders caused Salinger's Twelfth Infantry Regiment to be almost totally wiped out.

There is no doubt in my mind that Salinger felt bitter about these three disasters. He not only witnessed all three of them but he was almost killed at Slapton Sands. The flawed decisions of Moon, Bradley, and Gerow cost Salinger's Fourth Infantry Division several thousand casualties, including over a thousand deaths. It is therefore no wonder Salinger felt that there was no great difference between the bastards in the US Army and those among the Nazis.

Salinger does not give us examples of German generals corresponding to Moon, Bradley, and Gerow, but in his stories he mentions two of the top three Nazi leaders, Adolf Hitler and Joseph Goebbels. Salinger refers to Hitler in three of his stories.

Clockwise from top left: Admiral Moon, General Bradley, and General Gerow (National Archives)

Salinger's first story to mention Hitler is "Last Day of the Last Furlough" (1944). In that story, the central character, Babe Gladwaller, makes three statements about Hitler. Those statements suggest that Salinger had not been following the news stories about the Nazis' campaign to exterminate the entire Jewish population of Europe.

Gladwaller first mentions Hitler in a dinner table speech when he says that Hitler "provoked" World War II. When Salinger wrote that sentence about Hitler "provoking" World War II, he apparently was unaware that Hitler started the war with the invasion of Poland. Gladwaller mentions Hitler again

Nazi leaders Hitler, Göring, and Goebbels (FDR Presidential Library)

in his speech after he deplores the way his father's generation glorified World War I. Gladwaller says that if soldiers come back from World War II glorifying "heroism and cockroaches and foxholes and blood . . . then future generations will always be doomed to future Hitlers." Here Salinger suggests that Hitler was merely one in a series of similar dictators and not the mind that planned the extermination of all the Jews in Europe. And Gladwaller's third reference to Hitler occurs when he says, "If German boys had learned to be contemptuous of violence, Hitler would have had to take up knitting to keep his ego warm."[6]

Salinger's comments about Hitler knitting to keep his ego warm show that in late 1943 or early 1944, when Salinger wrote "The Last Day of the Last Furlough," he had not understood the evil that Hitler personified. By that time, the *Wehrmacht* had overrun most of Europe and the Nazis were deporting Jews to death camps in occupied Poland. This was widely known, but Salinger does not mention it in "Last Day of the Last Furlough." Instead, he describes Hitler only as a warmonger, a possible antecedent of other "future Hitlers."

Salinger's second story to refer to Hitler is the unpublished "The Magic Foxhole," which he wrote shortly after D-Day in 1944. In a conversation between two American soldiers who recently participated in the D-Day landings, one of them wonders if the invasion will prevent future wars in Europe. The other soldier says he isn't sure that it will because "maybe another guy like Hitler will crop up."[7] With the phrase "another guy like Hitler," Salinger again revealed that he considered Hitler a generic type of dictator and not the personification of evil.

The third story in which Salinger refers to Hitler is "A Girl I Knew" (1948). Once again it is an extremely brief reference. It occurs when the narrator of the story mentions that he was a college student on a field trip "about the same hour Hitler's troops were marching into Vienna." When Salinger wrote "A Girl I Knew" three years after the end of World War II, he no longer saw Hitler as merely an imperialist aggressor, as he did when he wrote "Last Day of the Last Furlough" and "The Magic Foxhole." This becomes clear when the narrator, a CIC agent, talks about interrogating a former member of the SS who mentions "what terrible things had been done to the Jews in Vienna." Also, later in the story Salinger refers to a Jewish family who had been killed in the Buchenwald concentration camp.[8] So Salinger's later comments about Hitler and the Nazis acknowledge the Nazis' mistreatment of Jews in post-Anschluss Austria and the murder of Jews at the Buchenwald concentration camp. But these are only indirect references to the Holocaust that do not hold Hitler responsible for it.

Even though Salinger had seen and smelled the charred bodies of Jewish prisoners at a concentration camp, he never acknowledged the magnitude of the destruction of humanity that Hitler had set in motion. In his 1992 book *Democide: Nazi Genocide and Mass Murder*, Rudolph Rummel presents statistics from all European countries involved in World War II. According to those figures, Hitler is responsible for the war deaths of 28 million soldiers and civilians and for the murder of another 21 million people who died in mass executions and concentration camps. Rummel writes: "In total, the war killed 28,736,000 Europeans, a fantastic number. But the democide of Hitler alone adds 20,946,00 more." Rummel's term *democide* not only includes the genocide of the Jews but also "the murder of hostages, reprisal raids, forced labor, 'euthanasia,' starvation, exposure, medical experiments, and terror bombing."[9] But Salinger apparently was not aware—perhaps because he didn't want to be—that there is no individual in the history of the world who is responsible for the deaths of more people than Hitler.

Salinger's only reference to the second most evil Nazi, Joseph Goebbels, reveals even less of his attitude toward the Nazis than his Hitler statements. It occurs in "For Esmé—With Love and Squalor" when Sergeant X arrests a minor official in the Nazi Party and finds in her possession "a book by Goebbels, entitled 'Die Zeit Ohne Beispiel' [The Time without Equal]."[10] Salinger does not comment on the content of the book, which is a collection of Goebbels's essays that celebrate the rise of the Nazi Party and the resurgence of Germany as a world power.

Nor does Salinger identify Goebbels as having been the most vicious enemy of the Jews among the Nazi leadership. Goebbels joined the Nazi Party in 1924 and became its minister of propaganda after the party came to power in 1933. A virulent anti-Semite, Goebbels immediately started attacking the Jews and suggested that a worldwide Jewish conspiracy was planning a war against Germany. In November 1938, he orchestrated the Kristallnacht. During this "Night of Broken Glass," the SA and other party hardliners destroyed 7,500 Jewish shops and burned down more than one hundred synagogues. In 1942 Goebbels helped formulate the plan for the "final solution of the Jewish problem," which was to deport all Jews to Poland and other eastern European countries recently overrun by the Wehrmacht. In a March 27, 1942, diary entry, Goebbels wrote that after the Jews had been deported, "60 percent of them will have to be liquidated, whereas only 40 percent can be used for forced labor."[11] In late April 1945, while Russian troops were fighting their way toward the bunker in Berlin where Hitler was about to kill himself, Goebbels' diaries show him unrepentant. After Hitler's suicide, Goebbels had his six children injected with poison and then shot his wife and himself.

Salinger never mentions the third big Nazi, Hermann Göring. But he should have mentioned him because after Hitler, Göring was the most powerful Nazi in Germany. In 1925 he became the first commander of the paramilitary SA and one of the leaders of the Nazi Party. In 1933, Göring created the Gestapo, the secret state police, and in 1935 he became the commander-in-chief of the new German air force (the Luftwaffe). In 1936 Hitler put Göring in charge of the four-year-plan to build up the German army to the point where it would be the strongest military force in Europe. And in 1941 Göring rose to the apex of his power when Hitler named him his deputy and successor.

Göring never made the kinds of anti-Semitic speeches that Hitler and Goebbels were infamous for, but he knew that top Nazi leaders met at the Wannsee Conference on January 20, 1942, to plan the total extermination of Europe's Jews. Roger Manvell and Heinrich Fraenkel, the authors of a Göring biography, report that members of Göring's economic staff were present at that conference and demanded "exemption for Jewish armament workers." Manvell and Fraenkel conclude that "there can be no doubt that Goering knew in principle that genocide was now the official practice."[12] Nevertheless, at the Nuremberg war crimes trials Göring claimed that he knew nothing about the death camps. He even asserted that the movie footage of the huge masses of corpses in the liberated concentration camps was fake. After Göring was sentenced to death by hanging, he followed Hitler and Goebbels's examples and committed suicide.

It is unusual that Salinger said next to nothing about Goebbels in his writings and nothing at all about Göring. But even more unusual is the fact that he did not mention the Holocaust in his comments about Hitler. When Salinger wrote "Last Day of the Last Furlough" and "The Magic Foxhole" in 1943 and 1944, he was appallingly uninformed about the Nazis. How could he have missed the December 1942 *New York Times* article about the Holocaust? In it the *New York Times* reprinted the declaration of the governments of the United States, the United Kingdom, and nine allied countries that alerted the world to the mass slaughter of Jews by the Nazis. The declaration describes the monstrous scale of the Nazis' extermination program when it states that by December of 1942, the Nazis had already murdered "hundreds of thousands of entirely innocent men, women and children."[13] Yet in "Last Day of the Last Furlough" and "The Magic Foxhole," Salinger refers to Hitler as though he were merely some run-of-the-mill power-hungry dictator.

As far as Salinger's comparison of bastards in the US Army to bastards among the Nazis is concerned, I believe that he did not realize how objectionable that comparison is. I also think he didn't realize it because he deliberately avoided thinking, talking, and writing about the Holocaust. The comparison of US and Nazi bastards is objectionable for two reasons. One reason is that it suggests the commanders in the US Army had a lot in common with the Nazis, whom they were doing their best to defeat. The other reason is that the comparison is disturbingly lopsided. It does not make sense to equate American commanders like Admiral Moon and generals Gerow and Bradley to Nazi generals. Yes, the American commanders' flawed decisions resulted in hundreds of unnecessary fatalities among their own troops, but Nazi generals were responsible for massacres in which tens of thousands of innocent civilians were butchered.[14]

Conclusion

In my research for this book, I found that four widely accepted assumptions about Salinger's military service and about his life in postwar Germany are incorrect. American military records, German archives, and Salinger's letters show that:

1. Salinger never fought on the front lines with the combat soldiers of the Twelfth Infantry Regiment. After the D-Day landings, Salinger came under fire from the Germans only infrequently because his CIC detachment did its work well behind the front lines.
2. Salinger's nervous breakdown shortly after the end of the war was therefore not due to battle fatigue. It was due to a number of different factors, but the trigger was his visit to the Kaufering concentration camp, where he saw and smelled the bodies of scores of Jewish prisoners who had been burned to death by the SS.
3. The German woman whom Salinger married soon after the war, Dr. Sylvia Luise Welter, was neither a low-level official in the Nazi Party nor even a member of the Party, and there is no proof of a Gestapo connection.
4. The breakup of the marriage was not due to Welter's alleged anti-Semitism. Salinger himself said that it was due to their incompatibility and to the fact that he was unable to do any writing during the eight months of their marriage.

With these erroneous assumptions out of the way, I can now summarize how Salinger's attitude toward the Nazis changed during and after the war and what the probable reasons are for these changes. Salinger's stories, letters, and public and private statements about the Nazis reveal two shifts in his attitude: One from oblivious unconcern to a gung-ho, kill-the-Nazis attitude and a second shift from there to a final nonjudgmental stance.

Young Salinger spent ten months in Austria and Poland, but he left Europe just before the Nazis' takeover of Austria. He therefore did not find out until after he returned to the United States that the Nazis had immediately begun to terrorize the Jews in Vienna. But even then, the nineteen-year-old Salinger was not concerned about the Nazis. If he had been concerned, he would have said something in the weekly pieces that he wrote for the college paper at Ursinus College or in conversations with his classmates.

Salinger's initial unconcern about the Nazis can be explained in terms of his secular Jewish upbringing and his wealthy parents' attempts to fit in with the Gentile upper class. They even told Salinger that he and his sister, Doris, "weren't really Jewish" because their mother was brought up a Catholic and only pretended to have converted to Judaism. This might be the reason why the nineteen-year-old Salinger was not interested in what the Nazis were doing to the Jews in Austria.

Salinger's unconcern about the Nazis continued after Hitler had started World War II and his troops had overrun most of Europe. It was during this time that Salinger published his first short stories in American magazines. Three of those early stories were about young men in the military, but they do not mention the Nazis or the war in Europe. When Salinger's first military story appeared in July 1941, the German Wehrmacht had already overrun Poland and marched into Paris. But it was not until 1944 that Salinger first mentioned the Nazis in his fiction.

There are three possible reasons for Salinger's continued unconcern. One of these reasons is Salinger's strategy of using the publication of magazine stories to become a famous writer. Because the magazines were looking for upbeat stories about the military, Salinger avoided mentioning the war in Europe. A second reason Salinger's early military stories do not mention the Nazis is the December 1941 Japanese attack on Pearl Harbor. That attack brought the United States into World War II, but it focused public attention on the Japanese rather than on the Nazis and their conquest of Europe. And the third reason Salinger ignored the Nazis for a long time is that he was so disappointed about not being admitted to officer candidate school that he began to develop a very adversarial attitude toward the US Army, and this resentment distracted his attention away from the Nazis.

The first turning point in Salinger's attitude toward the Nazis came in October 1943 after Salinger was assigned to the Counter Intelligence School in Fort Holabird, Maryland. There he found out that he would soon be deployed to Europe. It was during his time at Fort Holabird that Salinger wrote "Last

Day of the Last Furlough." In this story, Salinger's central character is a soldier who is waiting to be shipped out for duty in Europe. He has the same army ID number as Salinger, but he is not a CIC agent. He has been trained as a combat soldier, and he says that he believes "in killing Nazis, Fascists, and Japs."

After Salinger participated in the D-Day landings and had come under fire from the Germans, we would expect his stories to continue pushing the "kill-the Nazis" theme, but they do not. In the post–D-Day stories "The Magic Foxhole" and "A Boy in France," the enemy are not called Nazis or Germans but "Krauts," and they come across not as the cold-hearted master race portrayed in American wartime movies but as a disembodied natural force.

Even in his later stories, Salinger does not present us with fully developed pictures of individual Nazis. All we get are two vignettes in "A Girl I Knew" and "For Esmé—With Love and Squalor." One of the two Nazis is an SS sergeant and the other is a minor official in the Nazi Party. In these thumbnail sketches, the central characters are CIC agents like Salinger himself. One of the agents is remarkably nonjudgmental toward the SS soldier whom he interrogates, and the other agent shows surprising sympathy for the woman who was a Nazi Party official.

While Salinger's attitude toward the Nazis was softening, his attitude toward the US Army and the war was becoming increasingly negative. Beginning after the rejection of his two applications to officer candidate school, Salinger made more and more disparaging comments about US Army personnel, particularly about officers. He was especially severe about the incompetent captain in "Two Lonely Men," the hedonist colonel in "A Girl I Knew," and the publicity-seeking general in "Blue Melody."

Salinger's comments about the US Army in his stories and letters suggest that a major reason for his negative attitude was the three major military disasters he was involved in. The sloppy planning of the catastrophic practice exercise at Slapton Sands in England, the bombing of American troops by the US Air Force near Saint-Lô in France, and the obstinacy of an American general during the Battle of the Hürtgen Forest in Germany caused Salinger's Fourth Infantry Division several thousand unnecessary casualties, including over a thousand deaths. These self-inflicted losses must have suggested to Salinger that American generals had no more respect for the lives of their soldiers than the German generals did for the lives of theirs. Moreover, Salinger's portrayal of two American generals in "Blue Melody" and *The Catcher in the Rye* shows that he did not respect the leadership of the US Army.

Salinger made his most negative comments about the Army in a letter he wrote a week after the end of the war, in the 1948 story "Blue Melody," and three years later in *The Catcher in the Rye*. In the May 13, 1945, letter, Salinger said the war was "a tricky, dreary farce" and that his most casual thoughts about the army were "edgy with treason"; in "Blue Melody," he had his narrator say that what the US Army fought the war for was "Mom's apple pie, ice-cold beer, the Brooklyn Dodgers, and the Lux Theater of the Air"; and in *The Catcher in the Rye*, Holden Caulfield's brother D. B. says that "the Army was practically as full of bastards as the Nazis were."

Considering Salinger's critical attitude toward the US Army and his non-judgmental attitude toward the Nazis, it is no wonder that he did his postwar Nazi hunting only halfheartedly. His disdain for the army leadership must have been confirmed by the fact that the top brass made the CIC round up many hundreds of Nazi scientists and gave them stateside jobs in US weapons research while they punished many thousands of lesser Nazis in Germany by jailing them, firing them from their jobs, or imposing fines on them.

This hypocrisy helps explain why Salinger equated American and Nazi bastards. Nevertheless, by making that comparison Salinger reveals a stunning disregard for the reason World War II was fought. It is universally agreed that in World War II the United States and the Allies fought pure evil. This evil was most sickeningly evident in the Holocaust. But Salinger never directly mentions the Holocaust in any of his thirty-five published stories, and he makes only two brief references to Nazi concentration camps, one in the story "A Girl I Knew" and one in a conversation with his daughter, Margaret.

This lack of outrage about the Holocaust is almost incomprehensible because Salinger witnessed what the Holocaust was all about. When he walked into the abandoned concentration camp at Kaufering, he saw and smelled the charred bodies of eighty-six Jewish prisoners whom the SS had recently burned to death in their earthen huts. These charred corpses should have convinced Salinger that US Army bastards were by no stretch of the imagination as bad as Nazi bastards.

How to explain Salinger's lack of outrage? It is my opinion that long before his visit to the Kaufering concentration camp, Salinger was troubled by the hundreds of dead soldiers, American and German, that he saw each time he and other field agents of the CIC moved into areas where the fighting had just ended and they had to look for documents in abandoned Wehrmacht command posts and on the bodies of dead German soldiers. His mind might have developed a defense mechanism so he could function despite the carnage all around him. That defense mechanism seems to have been denial. And when he saw and smelled the burned corpses at the Kaufering camp, he might again have tried to blank out the horrors but was unable to. The result was his nervous breakdown less than two weeks later. But even after his nervous collapse, he was still in denial. He was exhibiting symptoms consistent with what psychiatrists call avoidant personality disorder. This would explain why he downplayed his own Jewishness, avoided Jewish themes in his fiction, and never mentioned the Kaufering concentration camp in his stories or letters.

When I began to study Salinger's attitude toward the Nazis, I had no idea what I would come up with. I certainly hoped to reach a different conclusion than I did. I am troubled by having to admit this, but my reading and rereading of Salinger's wartime fiction and his letters has convinced me that he did not identify with the six million Jews the Nazis murdered. Although Salinger did not deny the Holocaust, he definitely tried to ignore it.

Notes

Introduction

1. Gerden F. Johnson, History of the Twelfth Infantry Regiment in World War II (Boston: National Fourth [Ivy] Division Association, 1947), 347.

2. J. D. Salinger to Eberhard Alsen, April 19, 2001.

3. Felix Römer, *Kameraden: Die Wehrmacht von Innen* [Comrades: The German Army from the Inside] (Munich: Piper, 2012), 470, 478.

Chapter 1. A Secular Jewish Upbringing

1. Margaret Salinger, *Dream Catcher* (New York: Washington Square Press, 2000), 20.

2. Ibid., 29.

3. Ian Hamilton, *In Search of J. D. Salinger* (London: Heinemann, 1988), 19.

4. Ibid.

5. Margaret Salinger, *Dream Catcher*, 33.

6. Ibid., 21.

7. Ibid., 22.

8. Ibid.

9. The seven stories about members of the Glass Family are "A Perfect Day for Bananafish" (1948); "Down at the Dinghy" (1949); "Franny" (1955); "Raise High the Roof Beam, Carpenters" (1955); "Zooey" (1957); "Seymour: An Introduction" (1959); and "Hapworth 16, 1924" (1965).

10. J. D. Salinger, "Down at the Dinghy," *Harper's*. April 1949; reprinted in *Nine Stories* (New York: Bantam, 1964), 86.

11. Like Lionel Tannenbaum, young Salinger also ran away from home more than once. Margaret Salinger heard from her Aunt Doris that when Sonny was four years old, he and Doris had a fight, and "Sonny got so mad he packed his suitcase and ran

away. He was always running away. When Mother came home from shopping a few hours later, she found him in the lobby. He was dressed from head to toe in his Indian costume, long headdress and all." Margaret Salinger, *Dream Catcher*, 18.

Chapter 2. Salinger in Austria before the Nazi Takeover

1. Kenneth Slawenski, *J. D. Salinger: A Life* (New York: Random House, 2010), 22.

2. My information about the Nazi takeover of Austria comes from two sources: Jürgen Gehl, *Austria, Germany, and the Anschluss* (London: Oxford University Press, 1963), and Günter Bischof, Anton Pelinka, and Alexander Lassner, *The Dollfuss/Schuschnigg Era in Austria: A Reassessment* (New Brunswick, NJ: Transaction, 2003).

3. "Jews Humiliated by Vienna Crowds. Families Compelled to Scrub Streets," *New York Times*, March 16, 1938, B3. "Jews Scrub Streets of Vienna Inner City. Forced to Remove Crosses of Fatherland Front," *New York Times*, March 24, 1938, D5.

4. "Backstage with *Esquire*," *Esquire*, September 1941, 24.

5. J. D. Salinger, "Contributors," *Story*, September/October 1942, 26.

6. J. D. Salinger to Ernest Hemingway, July 1945. Unless otherwise noted, all letters I quote can be found in the Copyright Department of the National Archives, Washington, DC.

7. William Maxwell, "J. D. Salinger," *Book of the Month Club News*, July 1951, 6.

8. J. D. Salinger, "A Girl I Knew," *Good Housekeeping*, February 1948, 194.

9. "Gaff," *Ursinus Weekly*, October 10, 1938, 2.

10. J. D. Salinger, "J. D. S.'s The Skipped Diploma," *Ursinus Weekly*, October 17, 1938, 2.

11. Ian Hamilton, *In Search of J. D. Salinger* (London: Heinemann, 1988), 45.

12. J. D. Salinger, "The Young Folks," *Story*, March/April 1940, 30.

Chapter 3. Continued Unconcern about the Nazis

1. J. D. Salinger, "The Hang of It," *Collier's*, July 12, 1941, 22.

2. J. D. Salinger to Whit Burnett, December 11, 1941.

3. J. D. Salinger, "Personal Notes of an Infantryman," *Collier's*, December 12, 1942, 96.

4. J. D. Salinger, "Soft-Boiled Sergeant," *Saturday Evening Post*, April 15, 1944, 18.

5. Kenneth Slawenski, *J. D. Salinger: A Life* (New York: Random House, 2010), 53.

6. William Maxwell, "J. D. Salinger," *Book of the Month Club News*, July 1951, 6.

7. J. D. Salinger, "This Sandwich Has No Mayonnaise," *Esquire*, October 1945, 149.

8. J. D. Salinger to Whit Burnett, July 1, 1943.

9. J. D. Salinger, "Once a Week Won't Kill You," *Story*, November/December 1944, 24.

10. J. D. Salinger, "Two Lonely Men," unpublished story, Firestone Library, Princeton University.

11. "11 Allies Condemn Nazi War on Jews," *New York Times*, December 18, 1942, A1.

Chapter 4. Ready to Kill Nazis

1. J. D. Salinger, "Last Day of the Last Furlough," *Saturday Evening Post*, July 15, 1944, 62.
2. J. D. Salinger, "Soft-Boiled Sergeant," *Saturday Evening Post*, April 15, 1944, 82.
3. Salinger, "Last Day of the Last Furlough," 62.

Chapter 5. The Slapton Sands Disasters

1. The story of the friendly fire incident was first revealed in Nigel Lewis, *Channel Firing: The Tragedy of Exercise Tiger* (London: Viking, 1989), and the most detailed account of the torpedo attack appears in Ken Small, *The Forgotten Dead: Why 946 American Servicemen Died off the Coast of Devon in 1944—And the Man Who Discovered Their True Story* (London: Bloomsbury, 1988).
2. Small, *Forgotten Dead*, 18–19.
3. Lewis, *Channel Firing*, 264.
4. Ibid., 262.
5. Werner Kleeman with Elizabeth Uhlig, *From Dachau to D-Day* (Rego Park, NY: Marble House, 2006), 82.
6. J. D. Salinger, "For Esmé—With Love and Squalor," *New Yorker*, April 18, 1950; reprinted in *Nine Stories* (New York: Bantam, 1964), 88.
7. Ibid., 94.

Chapter 6. Under Fire from the Wehrmacht

1. Ann Bray et al., *History of the Counter Intelligence Corps in World War II*, vol. 14 (Fort Holabird, MD: United States Army Intelligence Center, 1959), 2.
2. At Slapton Sands, 551 members of the Fourth Infantry Division were killed.
3. Margaret Salinger, *Dream Catcher* (New York: Washington Square Press, 2000), 53.
4. Ibid., 60.
5. Jerry Salinger, "The Magic Foxhole," unpublished story, Firestone Library, Princeton University, 1.
6. Ibid.
7. Peter Liddle, ed., *D-Day by Those Who Were There* (Barnsley, UK: Pen and Sword, 2004), 100.
8. Gerden F. Johnson, *History of the Twelfth Infantry Regiment in World War II* (Boston: National Fourth [Ivy] Division Association, 1947), 58.
9. Salinger, "Magic Foxhole," 4.
10. Ibid., 6.
11. J. D. Salinger, "A Boy In France," *Saturday Evening Post*, March 31, 1945, 21.

12. J. D. Salinger to Whit Burnett, June 12, 1944 (postcard).

13. Oliver Appleton, Periodic Report, 9 June 1944, Fourth Division CIC Detachment, Record Group 407–304 INF (12), National Archives and Records Administration, College Park, MD.

14. J. D. Salinger to Whit Burnett, June 28, 1944.

15. J. D. Salinger, "For Esmé—With Love and Squalor," *New Yorker*, April 18, 1950; reprinted in *Nine Stories* (New York: Bantam, 1964), 110.

Chapter 7. Salinger's Job as a CIC Agent

1. Kenneth Slawenski, *J. D. Salinger: A Life* (New York: Random House, 2010), 93.

2. "Biographies, Headquarters Company, Period 1 Jan., '44 to Aug., '45," in *Fourth Infantry Division* (Baton Rouge, LA: United Sates Army, Fourth Infantry Division, 1946), 163.

3. Ann Bray et al., *History of the Counter Intelligence Corps in World War II*, vol. 13 (Fort Holabird, MD: United States Army Intelligence Center, 1959), 1.

4. CIC School, "Operations in France and the Lowlands," in *History and Mission of the Counter Intelligence Corps in World War II* (Fort Holabird, MD: Counter Intelligence Center, 1946), 38–39 (emphasis added).

5. Oliver Appleton, Periodic Report, June 8, 1944, Fourth Division CIC Detachment, Record Group 407–304 INF (12), National Archives and Records Administration, College Park, MD.

6. Appleton, Periodic Report, June 13, 1944.

7. Ibid.

8. J. D. Salinger to Frances "Terry" Glassmoyer, August 7, 1944, http://icollector .com/J-D-Salinger-ALS_i9781703.

9. J. D. Salinger, "Contributors," *Story*, November/December 1944, 41.

10. Werner Kleeman with Elizabeth Uhlig, *From Dachau to D-Day* (Rego Park, NY: Marble House Editions, 2006), 98.

Chapter 8. The Saint-Lô SNAFU and the Liberation of Paris

1. Geoffrey Regan, *Military Anecdotes* (London: Guinness, 1992), 33.

2. Martin Blumenson, *Breakout and Pursuit* (Washington, DC: Center of Military History, United States Army, 1993), 220–21.

3. Ibid., 229.

4. Ibid., 236–37.

5. John C. McManus, *The Americans at Normandy* (New York: Forge, 2004), 296–97.

6. James J. Carafano, *After D-Day: Operation Cobra and the Normandy Breakout* (Boulder, CO: Lynne Rienner, 2000), 118, 120.

7. Gerden F. Johnson, *History of the Twelfth Infantry Regiment in World War II* (Boston: National Fourth [Ivy] Division Association, 1947), 133.

8. J. D. Salinger to Whit Burnett, September 9, 1944.

9. Ernie Pyle, *Brave Men* (New York: Holt, 1944), 456.

10. J. D. Salinger to Whit Burnett, September 9, 1944.

11. John Skow, "Sonny—An Introduction," *Time*, September 15, 1961, 88.

12. Margaret Salinger, *Dream Catcher* (New York: Washington Square Press, 2000), 60.

13. Oliver Appleton, Periodic Report, June 22, 1944, Fourth Division CIC Detachment, Record Group 407-304 INF (12), National Archives and Records Administration, College Park, MD.

14. Ernest Hemingway to Malcolm Cowley, September 3, 1945, Ernest Hemingway Collection, John F. Kennedy Library, Boston.

Chapter 9. The Hürtgen Forest Fiasco

1. Charles B. MacDonald, *The Battle of the Huertgen Forest* (1963; reprint, Philadelphia: University of Pennsylvania Press, 2003), 205.

2. Omar Bradley, with Clay Blair, *A General's Life* (New York: Simon & Schuster, 1983), 343.

3. Gerden F. Johnson, *History of the Twelfth Infantry Regiment in World War II* (Boston: National Fourth [Ivy] Division Association, 1947), 204.

4. Ernest Hemingway, *Across the River and into the Trees* (New York: Scribner's, 1950), 227–28.

5. Johnson, *History of the Twelfth Infantry Regiment*, 212.

6. MacDonald, *Battle of the Huertgen Forest*, 139.

7. Johnson, *History of the Twelfth Infantry Regiment*, 208, 221–22.

8. Hemingway, *Across the River*, 228.

9. J. D. Salinger to Elizabeth Murray, November 28, 1944.

10. Werner Kleeman with Elizabeth Uhlig, *From Dachau to D-Day* (Rego Park, NY: Marble House, 2006), 285–86.

11. J. D. Salinger, "The Stranger," *Collier's*, December 1, 1945, 77.

12. Ibid.

Chapter 10. Searching for Nazi Spies and Collaborators in Luxembourg

1. Gerden F. Johnson, *History of the Twelfth Infantry Regiment in World War II* (Boston: National Fourth [Ivy] Division Association, 1947), 235.

2. Oliver Appleton, Periodic Report, December 7, 1944, Fourth Division CIC Detachment, Record Group 407-304 INF (12), National Archives and Records Administration, College Park, MD.

3. Ibid.

4. James L. Gilbert, John P. Finnegan, and Ann Bray, *In the Shadow of the Sphinx: A History of Army Counterintelligence* (Fort Belvoir, VA: History Office, US Army Intelligence and Security Command, 2005), 50.

5. Ibid.

6. Appleton, Periodic Report, December 22, 1944.

7. Appleton, Periodic Report, December 9, 1944.

8. Appleton, Periodic Report, January 1, 1945.

9. Johnson, *History of the Twelfth Infantry Regiment*, 287.

10. Leicester Hemingway, *My Brother Ernest Hemingway* (1961; reprint, Sarasota, FL: Pineapple Press, 1996), 264.

11. J. D. Salinger, "Blue Melody," *Cosmopolitan*, September 1948, 51.

12. Ibid.

Chapter 11. Visit to a Concentration Camp

1. Margaret Salinger, *Dream Catcher* (New York: Washington Square Press, 2000), 55.

2. Paul Fussell, *The Boys' Crusade: The American Infantry in Northwestern Europe, 1944–1945* (New York: Modern Library, 2003), 151–52.

3. Anton Posset, "Das Ende des Holocaust in Bayern" [The End of the Holocaust in Bavaria], *Landsberg im 20. Jahrhundert* 2 (1993): 32–33.

4. Anton Posset, "Die amerikanische Armee entdeckt den Holocaust" [The American Army Discovers the Holocaust], *Landsberg im 20. Jahrhundert* 2 (1993): 37.

5. Julien Saks, "GIs Discover Holocaust," in *Hellcats*, ed. Ken Bradstreet (Paducah, KY: Turner, 1987), 118.

6. Ibid., 117.

7. Louis P. Lochner, "U.S. Officer Makes Germans View Horror Scene," in *Hellcats*, ed. Ken Bradstreet (Paducah, KY: Turner, 1987), 116.

8. John D. McCallum and Charles Larson, *Crime Doctor* (Vancouver, BC: Gordon Soules, 1978), 58.

9. Posset, "Das Ende des Holocaust," 32.

10. Joseph Hausner, "Strafing and Liberation," www.12tharmoredmuseum.com.

11. *Dachau War Crimes Trials* [transcripts], War Crimes Branch, Records of the Office of the Judge Advocate General (Army), Record Group 153, National Archives and Records Administration, College Park, MD.

12. www.buergervereinigung-landsberg.de/geschichte/orginalfilm.htm.

13. J. D. Salinger, "A Girl I Knew," *Good Housekeeping*, February 1948, 196.

14. Albert G. Rosenberg, *The Buchenwald Report*, trans. David A. Hackett (Boulder, CO: Westview, 1995).

15. The original title of the story refers to the popular song "Wien, Wien, nur Du allein sollst stets die Stadt meiner Träume sein" (Vienna, Vienna, only you alone shall ever be the city of my dreams).

Chapter 12. Nervous Breakdown

1. Gerden F. Johnson, *History of the Twelfth Infantry Regiment in World War II* (Boston: National Fourth [Ivy] Division Association, 1947), 162.

2. Ernie Pyle, *Brave Men* (New York: Holt, 1944), 439.

3. Jerry Salinger, "The Magic Foxhole," unpublished story, Firestone Library, Princeton University, 7.

4. Subcommittee on Posttraumatic Stress Disorder of the Committee on Gulf War and Health, *Posttraumatic Stress Disorder: Diagnosis and Assessment* (Washington, DC: National Academic Press, 2006), 13.

5. American Psychiatric Association, *Diagnostic and Statistical Manual of Mental Disorders*, 5th edition (Washington, DC: American Psychiatric Association, 2013), 274, 278.

6. Stadtarchiv Nürnberg (Nuremberg City Archive), file number C 18/II.

7. Ernst Klee, *Das Personenlexikon zum Dritten Reich* [Dictionary of Persons in the Third Reich] (Frankfurt am Main: Fischer, 2003), 155.

8. J. D. Salinger to Ernest Hemingway, July 1945.

9. J. D. Salinger to Elizabeth Murray, May 13, 1945.

10. The US Army called those five campaigns Normandy, Northern France, Rhineland, Ardennes-Alsace, and Central Europe.

11. J. D. Salinger, "For Esmé—With Love and Squalor," *New Yorker*, April 18, 1950; reprinted in *Nine Stories* (New York: Bantam, 1964), 106.

12. Margaret Salinger, *Dream Catcher* (New York: Washington Square Press, 2000), 68.

13. J. D. Salinger, "A Perfect Day for Bananafish," *New Yorker*, January 31, 1948; reprinted in *Nine Stories* (New York: Bantam, 1964), 6.

14. J. D. Salinger, "Seymour: An Introduction," *New Yorker*, June 6, 1959; reprinted in *Raise High the Roof Beam, Carpenters and Seymour: An Introduction* (New York: Bantam, 1965), 114, 134.

15. Salinger, "Perfect Day for Bananafish," 6.

16. Johnson, *History of the Twelfth Infantry Regiment*, 127.

17. Paul Fussell, *Doing Battle: The Making of a Skeptic* (Boston: Little, Brown, 1983), 122.

18. Steven M. Southwick, Rachel Yehuda, and Earl L. Giller, "Personality Disorders in Treatment-Seeking Combat Veterans with Posttraumatic Stress Disorder," *American Psychiatry* 150, no. 7 (1993), 1021–22.

19. American Psychiatric Association, *Diagnostic and Statistical Manual of Mental Disorders*, 673.

20. Margaret Salinger, *Dream Catcher*, 428.

21. American Psychiatric Association, *Diagnostic and Statistical Manual of Mental Disorders*, 674.

Chapter 13. Was Salinger's German Wife a Nazi?

1. Ian Hamilton, *In Search of J. D. Salinger* (London: Heinemann, 1988), 97.

2. Margaret Salinger, *Dream Catcher* (New York: Washington Square Press, 2000), 71.

3. Richard Swift, letter to the editor, *Hendersonville Times-News*, July 24, 2007, online edition, www.blueridgenow.com/article/20070724/NEWS/707240326.

4. Fourth Infantry Division Operations Reports, S1 Report, May 16, 1945, Record Group 407-304 INF (12), National Archives and Records Administration, College Park, MD.

5. Earl F. Ziemke, *The U.S. Army in the Occupation of Germany, 1944–1946* (Washington, DC: Center of Military History, United States Army, 1975), 322.

6. "U.S. Army Ends Ban on German Brides," *New York Times*, December 12, 1946, L22.

7. Kenneth Slawenski, *J. D. Salinger: A Life* (New York: Random House, 2010), 142.

8. J. D. Salinger to Elizabeth Murray, December 30, 1945.

9. Bernd Noack, "J. D. Salinger in Deutschland: Gunzenhausens heimlicher Held" [J. D. Salinger in Germany: Gunzenhausen's Secret Hero], *Frankfurter Allgemeine Zeitung*, September 24, 2009, 32.

10. J. D. Salinger to Paul Fitzgerald, November 23, 1946, cited in David Shields and Shane Salerno, *Salinger* (New York: Simon & Schuster, 2013), 185–86.

11. J. D. Salinger to Elizabeth Murray, June 13, 1946.

12. Cited in Hamilton, *In Search of J. D. Salinger*, 86.

13. Shields and Salerno, *Salinger*, 186.

14. Klaus-Michael Mallman and and Gerhard Paul, "Omniscient, Omnipotent, Omnipresent? Gestapo, Society, and Resistance," in *Nazism and German Society, 1933–1945*, ed. David F. Crew (New York: Routledge, 1994), 166–96.

15. Walter Otto Weyrauch, "Gestapo Informants: Facts and Theory of Undercover Operations," *Columbia Journal of Transnational Law* 24 (1986), 553–96.

16. Noack, "J. D. Salinger in Deutschland," 32.

17. Günter Horn to Eberhard Alsen, Nuremberg, November 23, 2009.

18. Margaret Salinger, *Dream Catcher*, 71, 359.

Chapter 14. Half-Heartedly Hunting Nazis after the War

1. Reproduced in David Shields and Shane Salerno, *Salinger* (New York: Simon & Schuster, 2013), 108.

2. A translation of the *Fragebogen* questions can be found in Constantine FitzGibbon, *Denazification* (London: Joseph, 1969), 185–93.

3. Frederick Taylor, *Exorcising Hitler: The Occupation and Denazification of Germany* (London: Bloomsbury, 2011), 261.

4. Ann Bray et al., *History of the Counter Intelligence Corps in World War II*, vol. 27 (Fort Holabird, MD: United States Army Intelligence Center, 1959), 18.

5. Earl F. Ziemke, *The U.S. Army in the Occupation of Germany, 1944–1946* (Washington, DC: Center of Military History, United States Army, 1975), 394.

6. John Gimbel, *The American Occupation of Germany: Politics and Military, 1945–1949* (Stanford, CA: Stanford University Press, 1968), 102.

7. J. D. Salinger to Ernest Hemingway, July 1945.

8. J. D. Salinger to Elizabeth Murray, December 30, 1945.

9. J. D. Salinger, "A Girl I Knew," *Good Housekeeping*, February 1948, 194.

10. J. D. Salinger, "For Esmé—With Love and Squalor," *New Yorker*, April 18, 1950; reprinted in *Nine Stories* (New York: Bantam, 1964), 105.

11. J. D. Salinger, "A Girl I Knew," 195–96.

12. Linda Hunt, *Secret Agenda: The United States Government, Nazi Scientists, and Project Paperclip, 1945–1990* (New York: St. Martin's, 1991), 109.

13. Leon Jaroff, "The Rocket Man's Dark Side," *Time*, March 26, 2002. For Braun's presence at the torture and execution of prisoners by the SS, see Wayne Biddle, *Dark Side of the Moon: Wernher von Braun, the Third Reich, and the Space Race* (New York: Norton, 2009), 121–26.

14. Hunt, *Secret Agenda*, 39.

Chapter 15. American Bastards and Nazi Bastards

1. J. D. Salinger, *The Catcher in the Rye* (1951; New York: Bantam, 1964), 140.

2. J. D. Salinger, "Blue Melody," *Cosmopolitan*, September 1948, 51.

3. S. L. A. Marshall, *Bastogne: The Story of the First Eight Days* (Washington, DC: Zenger, 1979), 116–17.

4. Martin Blumenson, *The Patton Papers*, vol. 2. (Boston: Houghton-Mifflin, 1974), 744, 758, 751, 787.

5. Ibid., 333.

6. J. D. Salinger, "Last Day of the Last Furlough," *Saturday Evening Post*, July 15, 1944, 62.

7. Jerry Salinger, "The Magic Foxhole," unpublished story, Firestone Library, Princeton University, 6.

8. J. D. Salinger, "A Girl I Knew," *Good Housekeeping*, February 1948, 194, 196.

9. Rudolph J. Rummel, *Democide: Nazi Genocide and Mass Murder* (New Brunswick, NJ: Transaction, 1992), 11, 14.

10. J. D. Salinger, "For Esmé—With Love and Squalor," *New Yorker*, April 18, 1950; reprinted in *Nine Stories* (New York: Bantam, 1964), 105.

11. Joseph Goebbels, *The Goebbels Diaries, 1942–1943*, edited, translated, and with an introduction by Louis P. Lochner (Garden City, NY: Doubleday, 1948), 147–48.

12. Roger Manvell and Heinrich Fraenkel, *Goering* (New York: Simon & Schuster, 1962), 259–60.

13. "11 Allies Condemn Nazi War on Jews," *New York Times*, December 18, 1942, A1.

14. The worst Nazi massacres were the reprisals following the uprising in the Warsaw ghetto in August 1943. SS-Reichsführer Heinrich Himmler ordered that the population of Warsaw be completely exterminated. Under the command of SS General Erich von dem Bach-Zelewski, SS and Nazi police units murdered an estimated forty thousand civilians. See Richard C. Lukas, *The Forgotten Holocaust: The Poles under German Occupation, 1939–1944* (Lexington: University Press of Kentucky, 1986), 199–200; and Timothy Snyder, *Bloodlands: Europe between Hitler and Stalin* (New York: Basic Books, 2010), 304.

Bibliography

"11 Allies Condemn Nazi War on Jews." *New York Times*, December 18, 1942, A1.

American Psychiatric Association, Task Force on Nomenclature and Statistics. *Diagnostic and Statistical Manual of Mental Disorders*. 5th. ed. Washington, DC: American Psychiatric Association, 2013.

Appleton, Oliver. Periodic Reports of the Fourth Division CIC Detachment. June 1944 to May 1945. Record Group 407-304 INF (12). National Archives and Records Administration. College Park, MD.

"Backstage with Esquire." *Esquire*, September 1941, 24.

Biddle, Wayne. *Dark Side of the Moon: Wernher von Braun, the Third Reich, and the Space Race*. New York: Norton, 2009.

"Biographies, Headquarters Company, Period 1 Jan., '44 to Aug., '45." In *Fourth Infantry Division*, 162–64. Baton Rouge, LA: United States Army, Fourth Infantry Division, 1946.

Bischof, Günter, Anton Pelinka, and Alexander Lassner. *The Dollfuss/Schuschnigg Era in Austria: A Reassessment*. New Brunswick, NJ: Transaction, 2003.

Blumenson, Martin. *Breakout and Pursuit*. Washington, DC: Center of Military History, United States Army, 1993.

———. *The Patton Papers*, vol. 2. Boston: Houghton-Mifflin, 1974.

Böll, Heinrich. *And Where Were You, Adam?* 1951; reprint, Chicago: Northwestern University Press, 1994.

———. *The Train Was on Time*. 1949; reprint, New York: Little, Brown, 1967.

Bradley, Omar, and Clay Blair. *A General's Life*. New York: Simon & Schuster, 1983.

Bray, Ann, et al. *History of the Counter Intelligence Corps in World War II*. 30 vols. Fort Holabird, MD: United States Army Intelligence Center, 1959.

Carafano, James J. *After D-Day: Operation Cobra and the Normandy Breakout*. Boulder, CO: Lynne Rienner, 2000.

CIC School. "Operations in France and the Lowlands." In *History and Mission of the Counter Intelligence Corps in World War II.* Fort Holabird, MD: Counter Intelligence Center, 1946.

Dachau War Crimes Trials [Transcripts]. War Crimes Branch. Records of the Office of the Judge Advocate General (Army). Record Group 153. National Archives and Records Administration. College Park, MD.

FitzGibbon, Constantine. *Denazification.* London: Joseph, 1969.

Fourth Infantry Division Operations Reports. Record Group 407-304 INF (12). National Archives and Records Administration. College Park, MD.

Fussell, Paul. *The Boys' Crusade: The American Infantry in Northwestern Europe, 1944-1945.* New York: Modern Library, 2003.

———. *Doing Battle: The Making of a Skeptic.* Boston: Little, Brown, 1983.

"Gaff." *Ursinus Weekly,* October 10, 1938, 2.

Gehl, Jürgen. *Austria, Germany, and the Anschluss.* London: Oxford University Press, 1963.

Gilbert, James L., John P. Finnegan, and Ann Bray. *In the Shadow of the Sphinx: A History of Army Counterintelligence.* Fort Belvoir, VA: History Office, US Army Intelligence and Security Command, 2005.

Gimbel, John. *The American Occupation of Germany: Politics and Military 1945-1949.* Stanford, CA: Stanford University Press, 1968.

Goebbels, Joseph. *The Goebbels Diaries, 1942-1943.* Edited, translated, and with an introduction by Louis P. Lochner. Garden City, NY: Doubleday, 1948.

Hamilton, Ian. *In Search of J. D. Salinger.* London: Heinemann, 1988.

Hausner, Joseph. "Strafing and Liberation." www.12tharmoredmuseum.com.

Hemingway, Ernest. *Across the River and into the Trees.* New York: Scribner's, 1950.

———. *A Farewell to Arms.* New York: Scribner's, 1929.

———. *For Whom the Bell Tolls.* New York: Scribner's, 1940.

———. *In Our Time.* New York: Boni and Liveright, 1925.

———. Letter to Malcolm Cowley, September 3, 1945. Ernest Hemingway Collection. John F. Kennedy Library, Boston, MA.

Hemingway, Leicester. *My Brother Ernest Hemingway.* 1961; reprint, Sarasota, FL: Pineapple Press, 1996.

Horn, Günter. Letter to Eberhard Alsen, Nuremberg, November 20, 2009.

Hunt, Linda. *Secret Agenda: The United States Government, Nazi Scientists, and Project Paperclip, 1945-1990.* New York: St. Martin's, 1991.

Jaroff, Leon. "The Rocket Man's Dark Side." *Time,* March 26, 2002, 27.

"Jews Humiliated by Vienna Crowds. Families Compelled to Scrub Streets." *New York Times,* March 16, 1938, B3.

"Jews Scrub Streets of Vienna Inner City. Forced to Remove Crosses of Fatherland Front." *New York Times,* March 4, 1938, D5.

Johnson, Gerden F. *History of the Twelfth Infantry Regiment in World War II.* Boston: National Fourth [Ivy] Division Association, 1947.

Klee, Ernst. *Das Personenlexikon zum Dritten Reich* [Dictionary of Persons in the Third Reich]. Frankfurt am Main: Fischer, 2003.

Kleeman, Werner, with Elizabeth Uhlig. *From Dachau to D-Day*. Rego Park, NY: Marble House, 2006.

Lewis, Nigel. *Channel Firing: The Tragedy of Exercise Tiger*. London: Viking, 1989.

Liddle, Peter, ed. *D-Day by Those Who Were There*. Barnsley, UK: Pen and Sword, 2004.

Lochner, Louis P. "U.S. Officer Makes Germans View Horror Scene." In *Hellcats*, ed. Ken Bradstreet. Paducah, KY: Turner, 1987.

Lukas, Richard C. *The Forgotten Holocaust: The Poles under German Occupation, 1939–1944*. Lexington: University Press of Kentucky, 1986.

MacDonald, Charles B. *The Battle for the Huertgen Forest*. 1963; reprint, Philadelphia: University of Pennsylvania Press, 2003.

Mallman, Klaus-Michael, and Gerhard Paul. "Omniscient, Omnipotent, Omnipresent? Gestapo, Society, and Resistance." In *Nazism and German Society, 1933–1945*, ed. David F. Crew, 166–96. New York: Routledge, 1994.

Manvell, Roger, and Heinrich Fraenkel. *Goering*. New York: Simon & Schuster, 1962.

Marshall, S. L. A. *Bastogne: The Story of the First Eight Days*. Washington, DC: Zenger, 1979.

Maugham, Somerset. *The Razor's Edge*. 1944; reprint, New York: Vintage, 1972.

Maxwell, William. "J. D. Salinger." *Book of the Month Club News*, July 1951, 5–6.

McCallum, John D., and Charles P. Larson. *Crime Doctor*. Vancouver, BC: Gordon Soules, 1978.

McManus, John C. *The Americans at Normandy*. New York: Forge, 2004.

Noack, Bernd. "J. D. Salinger in Deutschland: Gunzenhausens heimlicher Held" [J. D. Salinger in Germany: Gunzenhausen's Secret Hero]. *Frankfurter Allgemeine Zeitung*. September 24, 2009, 32.

Posset, Anton. "Das Ende des Holocaust in Bayern" [The End of the Holocaust in Bavaria]. *Landsberg im 20. Jahrhundert* 2 (1993): 24–34.

———. "Die amerikanische Armee entdeckt den Holocaust" [The American Army Discovers the Holocaust]. *Landsberg im 20. Jahrhundert* 2 (1993): 35–41.

Pyle, Ernie. *Brave Men*. New York: Holt, 1944.

Regan, Geoffrey. *Military Anecdotes*. London: Guinness, 1992.

Römer, Felix. *Kameraden: Die Wehrmacht von Innen* [Comrades: The German Army from Inside]. Munich: Piper, 2012.

Rosenberg, Albert G. *The Buchenwald Report*. Trans. David A. Hackett. Boulder, CO: Westview, 1995.

Rummel, Rudolph J. *Democide: Nazi Genocide and Mass Murder*. New Brunswick, NJ: Transaction, 1992.

Saks, Julien. "GIs Discover Holocaust." In *Hellcats*, ed. Ken Bradstreet. Paducah, KY: Turner, 1987.

Salerno, Shane, dir. *Salinger*. The Story Factory, 2013. Film.

Salinger, J. D. "Blue Melody." *Cosmopolitan*, September 1948, 51, 112–19.

———. "A Boy in France." *Saturday Evening Post*, March 31, 1945, 21, 92.

———. *The Catcher in the Rye*. 1951; reprint, New York: Bantam, 1964.

———. "Contributors." *Story*, September/October 1942, 2.

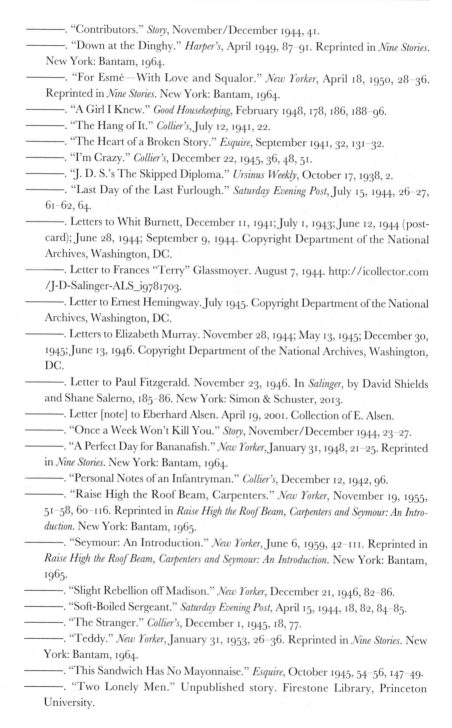

————. "Contributors." *Story*, November/December 1944, 41.

————. "Down at the Dinghy." *Harper's*, April 1949, 87–91. Reprinted in *Nine Stories*. New York: Bantam, 1964.

————. "For Esmé—With Love and Squalor." *New Yorker*, April 18, 1950, 28–36. Reprinted in *Nine Stories*. New York: Bantam, 1964.

————. "A Girl I Knew." *Good Housekeeping*, February 1948, 178, 186, 188–96.

————. "The Hang of It." *Collier's*, July 12, 1941, 22.

————. "The Heart of a Broken Story." *Esquire*, September 1941, 32, 131–32.

————. "I'm Crazy." *Collier's*, December 22, 1945, 36, 48, 51.

————. "J. D. S.'s The Skipped Diploma." *Ursinus Weekly*, October 17, 1938, 2.

————. "Last Day of the Last Furlough." *Saturday Evening Post*, July 15, 1944, 26–27, 61–62, 64.

————. Letters to Whit Burnett, December 11, 1941; July 1, 1943; June 12, 1944 (postcard); June 28, 1944; September 9, 1944. Copyright Department of the National Archives, Washington, DC.

————. Letter to Frances "Terry" Glassmoyer. August 7, 1944. http://icollector.com /J-D-Salinger-ALS_i9781703.

————. Letter to Ernest Hemingway. July 1945. Copyright Department of the National Archives, Washington, DC.

————. Letters to Elizabeth Murray. November 28, 1944; May 13, 1945; December 30, 1945; June 13, 1946. Copyright Department of the National Archives, Washington, DC.

————. Letter to Paul Fitzgerald. November 23, 1946. In *Salinger*, by David Shields and Shane Salerno, 185–86. New York: Simon & Schuster, 2013.

————. Letter [note] to Eberhard Alsen. April 19, 2001. Collection of E. Alsen.

————. "Once a Week Won't Kill You." *Story*, November/December 1944, 23–27.

————. "A Perfect Day for Bananafish." *New Yorker*, January 31, 1948, 21–25. Reprinted in *Nine Stories*. New York: Bantam, 1964.

————. "Personal Notes of an Infantryman." *Collier's*, December 12, 1942, 96.

————. "Raise High the Roof Beam, Carpenters." *New Yorker*, November 19, 1955, 51–58, 60–116. Reprinted in *Raise High the Roof Beam, Carpenters and Seymour: An Introduction*. New York: Bantam, 1965.

————. "Seymour: An Introduction." *New Yorker*, June 6, 1959, 42–111. Reprinted in *Raise High the Roof Beam, Carpenters and Seymour: An Introduction*. New York: Bantam, 1965.

————. "Slight Rebellion off Madison." *New Yorker*, December 21, 1946, 82–86.

————. "Soft-Boiled Sergeant." *Saturday Evening Post*, April 15, 1944, 18, 82, 84–85.

————. "The Stranger." *Collier's*, December 1, 1945, 18, 77.

————. "Teddy." *New Yorker*, January 31, 1953, 26–36. Reprinted in *Nine Stories*. New York: Bantam, 1964.

————. "This Sandwich Has No Mayonnaise." *Esquire*, October 1945, 54–56, 147–49.

————. "Two Lonely Men." Unpublished story. Firestone Library, Princeton University.

————. "The Young Folks." *Story*, March/April 1940, 26–30.

Salinger, Jerry. "The Magic Foxhole." Unpublished story. Firestone Library, Princeton University.

Salinger, Margaret. *Dream Catcher*. New York: Washington Square Press, 2000.

Shields, David, and Shane Salerno. *Salinger*. New York: Simon & Schuster, 2013.

Skow, John. "Sonny—An Introduction." *Time*, September 15, 1961, 84–90.

Slawenski, Kenneth. *J. D. Salinger: A Life*. New York: Random House, 2010.

Small, Ken. *The Forgotten Dead: Why 946 American Servicemen Died off the Coast of Devon in 1944—And the Man Who Discovered Their True Story*. London: Bloomsbury, 1988.

Snyder, Timothy. *Bloodlands: Europe between Hitler and Stalin*. New York: Basic Books, 2010.

Southwick, Steven M., Rachel Yehuda, and Earl Giller. "Personality Disorders in Treatment-Seeking Veterans with Posttraumatic Stress Disorder." *American Journal of Psychiatry* 150, no. 7 (1993): 1020–23.

Stephan, Jan. Transcript of an unpublished interview with Bernhard Horn and Günther Horn, cousins of Sylvia Luise Welter. Nuremberg, October 1, 2009.

Subcommittee on Posttraumatic Stress Disorder of the Committee on Gulf War and Health. *Posttraumatic Stress Disorder: Diagnosis and Assessment*. Washington, DC: National Academic Press, 2006.

Swift, Richard. Letter to the editor. *Hendersonville Times-News*, July 24, 2007. Online edition. www.blueridgenow.com/article/20070724/NEWS/707240326.

Taylor, Frederick. *Exorcising Hitler: The Occupation and Denazification of Germany*. London: Bloomsbury, 2011.

"U.S. Army Ends Ban on German Brides." *New York Times*, December 12, 1946, L22.

Weyrauch, Walter Otto. "Gestapo Informants: Facts and Theory of Undercover Operations." *Columbia Journal of Transnational Law* 24 (1986): 553–96.

Ziemke, Earl F. *The U.S. Army in the Occupation of Germany, 1944–1946*. Washington, DC: Center of Military History, United States Army, 1975.

Index